MY HUSBAND HAS ADD

and the Miraculous Discovery that Changed Our Life

A Memoir by
Linda Rosenbaum

TABLE OF CONTENTS

PREFACE

My husband Bob is intelligent, good looking, witty, loving, and has ADD. Ouch! That last one hurt. If you know little of what living with Adult ADD can lead to, by the end of this narrative you will be thoroughly enlightened.

Initially, I planned this story to be a legacy for our five grandchildren. I wanted them to have a sense of our family history and an understanding of how ADD (Attention Deficit Disorder) affects families like ours—those that have this gene.

Then I thought ... why not share my knowledge with others as well? After all, I have five decades of personal experience, based on living with a husband and a son who have ADD. I would have been immensely grateful for such an informative book fifty years ago.

Unfortunately, no such literature existed back then, as Adult ADD had not yet been acknowledged. Since few ADD marriages last fifty years, I realized I was in a unique position to educate others and demonstrate that they are not alone.

I began writing and almost immediately

became apprehensive. How could I expose our personal problems and humiliations to the world? I soon reconsidered abandoning this undertaking, and did.

But when I showed the partial manuscript to my husband's psychologist in 2010, he encouraged me to continue, stating that I would be helping many thousands. I was still hesitant. But shortly after that, major ADD issues I thought to be under control reappeared. Thus, in spite of my many qualms, I suddenly felt compelled to share this memoir with a wider audience after all. It has been an emotional and humbling experience to write about our journey.

By exposing details of our dismal life, beyond the textbook descriptions of ADD, I sincerely hope it will lead to accelerated research resulting in significant changes for those who suffer from this misunderstood disorder.

INTRODUCTION

According to a recent article in the *Wall Street Journal*[1] at least ten million adults in the United States have ADD (Attention Deficit Disorder), but only a quarter of them know or suspect they have it. Since knowledge is power, imagine how empowering it would be for the other seven and a half million to recognize, accept, and seek help for it.

Although ADHD is often referred to as the hyperactive type of ADD, the two are really one-and-the-same. All afflicted seem to have some form of hyperactivity, such as fidgeting, agitation, anger, and even tantrums.

As I researched and began writing this book, many people confessed to me that they or a loved one have ADD. Listening to their stories, I realized that the stigma of this brain disorder was fading fast, and that significantly more than the estimated ten million people are probably living with this condition. As those affected procreate and pass on this gene, the ADD population will continue to expand beyond belief.

---

[1] "Mind games: Attention Deficit Disorder isn't just for kids. Why adults are now being diagnosed, too." *Wall Street Journal,* April 6, 2010.

This narrative exposes little known truths regarding Adult ADD. Only individuals who have lived with such a person could describe their bizarre and often selfish behavior exhibited on a daily basis.

I have been married to Bob since 1960. He was not diagnosed until decades later, but has suffered from ADD-caused problems throughout his life. Many people, including some professionals, mistakenly dismiss this insidious devastating brain dysfunction as only a focusing and self-disciplining issue, when in reality it involves so much more.

ADD is not contagious, but it is inherited. One of our two children has it, as do two of our five grandchildren. It will no doubt have an impact on many Rosenbaum descendants forever. That fact alone is one of great sadness to me.

Whether aware, unaware, or in denial, this "demon" has the power to cause those afflicted, and more notably those close to them, a life of anguish and hardship. Since the affected walk among us and look perfectly normal, it is sometimes called the "hidden handicap." ADD children grow up to become ADD adults—and that folks is when the really big problems begin. "Little kids, little problems; big kids...." well, there is no time out corner for grown-ups!

Recognize this as a serious concern, and if needed, seek help, but only from a practitioner extremely well versed in the adult version of ADD.

Reading our intricate life story, you may wonder why I did not leave my husband. I often asked myself that question, but the answer is quite complex and the reasons vary greatly, often dependent upon the time and circumstances.

As to why I married Bob ... it was because I loved him. He was then, and still is my soul mate. That has never changed. Before we married, he was my mentor, believing in me when I did not always believe in myself. Although my self-esteem was not the best, he saw beyond that and convinced me that I was wise beyond my years.

The "new me" quickly blossomed as I successfully practiced standing up for myself against anyone who tried to take advantage of my gentle nature. I think his loving encouragement provided me with the backbone I was going to need to navigate through the complicated life I was about to lead. At that time, neither of us were remotely familiar with this disorder and its ramifications.

Although I am a victim of the consequences of Bob's affliction, he is clearly a victim as well. This condition has prevented him from living life with ease and genuine independence.

Beyond the commonly known attention deficit symptom, this memoir exposes other important characteristics that few have talked about ... until now. Bob has bravely offered to be the “Poster Adult” for ADD.

Those with thoughts of a relationship or marriage to such a person should look at this account as a cautionary tale. There are various symptoms as well as degrees of severity within this condition. They are discussed everywhere now: books, television, magazines, and blogs. Since the stigma has diminished and knowledge has increased, more are willing to take medications, which do help, but certainly not one hundred percent. Don’t expect perfection. If there is an ADD person you wish to keep in your life, be prepared to frequently practice the art of forgiveness.

Until now, and by design, only a few very close friends (and no extended family) were privy to our extreme difficulties caused by this handicap. By sharing this account, I hope to make a difference. This book is meant to reach the depth of the souls who need it most.

My intention is to offer knowledge, wisdom, and creative solutions to those afflicted, as well as those who live with or interact with them daily at home, work, or school. Much is possible for open-minded individuals.

After absorbing the realities of this educational chronicle, with disturbing and sometimes shocking ADD-caused situations, it will be uplifting to read about our discovery in 2011 that healed Bob and brought peace and harmony into our life.

Chapter 1
In the Beginning

Everything seemed perfect! There we were in 1960 ... beginning our life together as happy newlyweds. My husband Bob was twenty-two, and I was a young lady of eighteen. In my wildest dreams I could not have imagined the path our life would take, nor the mental pain, torment, and frustration I would endure over the next fifty years. I had not a clue that I had invited a "demon" of sorts into my life, as well as the future lives of many of our descendants for generations to come.

Unfortunately, Bob is afflicted with ADD. Although we knew nothing then of such a mental health issue, this challenging and disabling condition was to become the controlling force in every facet of our life, and mostly not in a good way.

We met on a blind date in December 1958 and realized almost immediately that we were meant to be. We spent as much time as possible together even though Bob was finishing his senior year of college in Connecticut and I was still in high school in Rhode Island. He was so totally absorbed with me that his grades slipped a bit, a significant change for him as he had always been a top honor student. But, I had become the main focus of his life, which made me very happy.

We were engaged in December 1959 and our beautiful wedding was celebrated in July 1960. We were in love and sharing dreams of "forever-together'. Bob was working at his first job as an electrical engineer in Massachusetts. Life was good.

Fast forward to the birth of our daughter Ava[2] in August 1961. Bob, who was totally devoted to me through that first year of marriage, began tracking labor pains as I was about to deliver. Since I was in labor for almost forty-three hours this involved a whole lot of tracking! Bob logged every contraction with the time and intensity as well as a description of how I was feeling (Not so good, thanks!). When the doctor inquired about my progress, Bob was able to hand over a huge document, not leaving out a single detail.

Who does this for almost two days—nonstop? Although I considered this merely a case of overkill at that time, it was really an example of intense ADD hyper-focusing.

So, our beautiful baby girl was born, and naturally we lived happily ever after ... at least that was the plan.

We moved when our baby was six weeks old. Bob decided he needed a more lucrative position, and found one in Rhode Island. We rented a home about twenty minutes from my

---

[2] Name has been changed for privacy.

mother and dad, who happily offered babysitting services as needed.

We had now been married fifteen months and Bob's demeanor began to change. Although I did not understand what was happening, nor attach any name to it, ADD had indeed reared its ugly head. Thus began my new and demanding life as Bob's mentally stressed enabler and mentor.

CHAPTER 2 – THE 60S
FUNKY DANCE

The 60s were a turbulent time with family values changing all over America. Terrible tragedies happened, including the assassinations of President Kennedy, Senator Kennedy, and Martin Luther King. Baby Boomers went wild at Woodstock. On a more personal level, this decade was also the start of stressful life changes in our household.

During our second year of marriage, Bob's personality began transforming. He developed strange ways of handling things.

On multiple occasions, his new demeanor and poor decisions puzzled me; often leaving me overwhelmed with frustration and anger. I have since learned that this is a common scenario, and the typical timeframe in an ADD marriage for symptoms to surface. (The level of "feel good" dopamine to the brain is elevated during the excitement of a new love, and then diminishes greatly as the normal responsibilities of life begin.)

We both unwittingly played our new roles well. For Bob, the hyper-focusing on a new relationship settled down as his offensive behavior suddenly erupted. For my part, I automatically slipped into a survival mode, attempting to create a normal lifestyle for us and our new baby.

In late 1961, living in Rhode Island, we had many new responsibilities as well as a baby daughter to tend to. Bob was commuting to work about forty-five minutes away. Three nights weekly he went directly from work to classes at Northeastern University in Boston working towards his master's degree. On those days he would leave early in the morning and return home at eleven o'clock in the evening. The fact that he was grouchy, impatient, and quite testy to all with whom he came in contact seemed like a natural result of his extremely busy schedule. Although this was a stressful lifestyle, it occurred to me that many endure such a grueling schedule to achieve their dreams without alienating most of the people in their lives.

I kept feeling that, in spite of his situation, his reactions to even minor events were overblown. He complained about everything, and the resulting tension building in our household left me feeling edgy most of the time. Where did the nice man who adored me go? The one who hyper-focused on me and never said an unkind word to me? He was swiftly and simply gone.

I know now that this change did not happen because he was so unhappy with any specific thing or even me, but he was so impatient and agitated, and every little thing seemed to make him irritable. I never knew what his trigger would be. He simply could not control his unruly agitation. He also seemed unable to place his focus anywhere and this behavior became habitual. It would, in fact, be many years before I would learn about the focusing and hyper-focusing involved in ADD. In any case, although I know he never deliberately intended to do so, he began to cause me untold mental stress and bewilderment.

About this time, Bob mentioned that he would like to move to a remote island and just live off the land alone with me. I knew he meant it, too. What, no stores, friends and family? No way. I love being with people.

But he brought up that scenario often, and I came to realize that he felt if we lived alone, just the two of us together, he would not have to worry or ever think about social situations that always caused him a great deal of anxiety. He never quite understood the protocol of acceptable social behavior.

At this point, having family or friends over for a visit became difficult. Bob either rambled on or lectured people on his thoughts and theories, most often on subjects no one else much cared about. On such subjects—how the Aborigines lived or something equally irrelevant—he would ramble to anyone in his vicinity. This was when I first realized that he mistook courtesy for interest. He would not stop talking and no one could get a word in edgewise. I knew this was not normal, but I had no idea why he did it.

Finally, when he became exceedingly rude to my family and friends, I stopped socializing, and that helped keep him calm. He seemed to be comfortable only with me. Often he would tell me he felt like he was from another planet, and frankly, I was beginning to believe he just might be! I never discussed any of this with anyone. I would not even know how to describe what was happening.

Adding to this, he constantly complained about the annoying things everyone around him did. That really puzzled me since he did most of those same annoying things himself. However, if I mentioned that fact, he would become angry and say, “You’re always picking on me.”

Confused, angry, and disgusted, all I could do was wonder why my husband was so unaware of his horrendous behavior.

As rude as he often was to my mother and dad, they no doubt, for my sake, quietly tolerated his conduct, and did so with amazing style and grace. I look back now on that time with great respect for them doing so. Bob was usually calm with my dad, but he and my mother always treaded on the edge of an argument. I often felt they were both at fault. They never agreed on much, and this just added to my stress.

****

Our second year in Rhode Island brought more change. Bob, always an excellent student but now working full time, was struggling to earn his masters degree in electrical engineering, a challenge under the best of circumstances.

Then unexpectedly, his folks who lived in Connecticut decided to visit on an important study weekend, against his wishes. They wanted to see their granddaughter, and no, the following weekend would simply not do! They would not take *no* for an answer. This was critical. Bob needed the weekend to study to get the required grades to continue in graduate school. Their selfishness ruined his study time, resulting in poor scores, which encouraged him to drop out of school.

They did not really care. I knew this was not a normal attitude for loving parents. But they had never been very supportive or caring. His dad was an angry man, always grouchy and insulting to everyone.

I began to realize that Bob had been raised in a dysfunctional family environment, and had unfortunately taken on many of his dad's unacceptable traits. To this day, our children remember their paternal grandfather as scary and mean. I realize now that Bob's dad had ADD. As an inherited trait, this was the legacy he unknowingly passed on to his son.

Later that year Bob became very restless in his job and said he wanted to look for new employment as soon as possible, but not in

Rhode Island. He wanted to get away from friends, family, and even the crazy drivers. (He was one of them, too, but in denial.)

I agreed to move and expected him to get newspapers from neighboring states and begin searching immediately. Weeks went by and he never bought a paper, but continued to complain about how miserable he was. I became miserable, too. What was going on with this man?

Thus began our funky dance—one that has stood the test of time, becoming the backbone of our survival for many decades. I named this dance routine, "Bob Breaks/ Linda Fixes."

I realized there would never be a new job unless I got things started. For several Sundays, I went to the local newsstand and gathered papers from all the surrounding states. Bob never looked at them. Strange! He was the one desperately wanting a new job. I started circling the engineering ads I thought might be appropriate. He briefly looked at them, but still he did nothing.

I wrote his resume and all the necessary cover letters, but could go no further. Only Bob could appear for the interviews.

Finally, with great reluctance and "strong prodding" from me, he began participating in his own job search. He eventually accepted a good offer as a design engineer from a company in Hartford, Connecticut.

Now certified as his official "enabler," I took

on this lifelong position with no retirement options. Over the years, I continuously performed this service, literally for my own survival and wellbeing and that of our family.

****

We moved to a suburb in the Hartford area in December 1962, settling into a small apartment. Six months later, we rented a larger three-bedroom house. We diligently saved our money so that eighteen months later we were able to build our first home.

I enjoyed good friendships, as I did wherever we lived, and we, as a couple, socialized often with neighbors.

As we approached the four-year mark in our peaceful little town, everything seemed to be working well for both of us. Ava was in nursery school, and I kept busy caring for our son Scott[3], born in October 1963. I felt amazingly secure, and was thoroughly enjoying my long-time favorite hobby—decorating-on-a-shoestring budget. Bob and I both appreciated the results of our efforts to build just the right home for our family. Life seemed rather stable.

Then, out of the blue, Bob said we would be moving to New Jersey. I was shocked! I could not imagine what prompted such thinking.

Bob claimed that with few engineering jobs

---

[3] Name changed for privacy.

in Connecticut, he felt insecure. He worried: What if he lost his job? He wanted to live in a state that offered ample opportunities should he become unemployed. I did not want to leave Connecticut and the good life I had worked so hard to create, but Bob insisted, and no discussion was possible. He was adamant. Quickly and impulsively he found an engineering position in central New Jersey with a company that would pay for our move. Reluctantly, at least for me, we put our year old home on the market and sold it in one week. New Jersey, here we come! The year was 1966.

Our newly built residence was not quite ready as we were loading up our moving van, but after some serious begging, the builder let us move in anyhow. The original closing date had to be postponed for one month, and we paid the builder rent for that time.

Then, only three weeks after we moved, the unbelievable did happen! Bob was laid off even before we closed on our home. In spite of the company's desire to hire him and pay for our move, they shut down that division, just like that! There we were, jobless, and about to close on a home we had already moved into. That only made me more homesick for the secure Connecticut homestead we had just left behind. We made no mention of being unemployed and quietly closed on our home a week later.

Bob was correct though about lots of job

opportunities in New Jersey. Within a couple of weeks he was again working—until that company moved to California a couple of years later. He then found another job, but two years after that he became a victim of their massive layoff. Leaving Connecticut had clearly not been a good decision, and New Jersey never felt like home to us.

Ironically, only a couple of months after we relocated to New Jersey, the Connecticut company Bob abandoned (after four and a half successful years) moved just two miles from our former home and remains there today. Additionally, new industries moved to the area, offering more engineering opportunities as well. Bob had not checked out any potential possibilities before impulsively uprooting us. He seemed to live within the realm of two speeds: procrastination and impulsiveness.

Other problems began to surface during our time in New Jersey. Our son Scott started throwing violent temper tantrums. When in kindergarten and first grade, I dreaded his return from school. He hated to change out of his school clothes, which was the normal custom of the day. My reminders to do so triggered such anger that often he would tear his room to shreds, stamp on the floor, and scream. (It would be many years before I realized ADD was the culprit). His teachers said he was not a discipline problem in school, but he lacked focus and enthusiasm when it came to learning. Bob had no patience or tolerance for Scott's antics and punished him all the time.

I often fantasized about escaping from the many stresses in my home, but of course, I knew that was not possible. I had no personal funds, nowhere to go, nor would I ever leave my children. I instead focused on creating stability for them and keeping our family intact. There was little quality "think-time" for me during this decade, and I was still only in my twenties when it ended.

I spent those youthful years grappling with Bob's new and confusing personality, giving birth twice, and moving seven times to accommodate multiple jobs in four different states. While I most certainly did not cherish Bob during the many episodes of turmoil he created, I instinctively knew that the man I fell in love with was still lurking somewhere within, and I was hopeful of eventually finding the answer to his mysterious behavior. He had never stopped loving me, of that I was absolutely certain.

For many women today, it would be absurd to think of remaining in such a distressing relationship. However, in the 60s and 70s a huge percentage of married women were homemakers and stay-at-home mothers. That was "the deal" we signed on for. Many of us depended on our husbands to be the breadwinners. Divorce was not common, however honoring marriage vows was.

Additionally, without a job, and the potential stigma of a failed marriage, women generally stayed put. Realize that this was the norm *then*, although very different from society today.

It was almost unheard of at that time for a woman to seek professional counseling, and doing so would not have helped me anyhow. Adult ADD was not yet known to anyone, including psychiatrists and clergy. During this chauvinistic period, most professionals would likely have advised me to go home and "be nicer" to my husband, implying that I was the one at fault! Leaving my marriage would only have added further complications to my already troubled life.

After four long years in New Jersey, and with Bob unemployed again, we were both quite eager to return to Connecticut. We put our home up for sale with a promise in writing from the realtor that he would purchase it if it did not sell. It did not, and he bought it as agreed. We received a fair price and ended up with a decent profit.

Meanwhile, Bob hastily accepted the first Connecticut position offered, this time in the New London area. *Déjà vu.* We bought a newly built home, moved in, and bam ... only weeks later Bob was unemployed again. Seven jobs in ten years! This was such a wearisome decade. The year was 1970.

ADD Notes

Those with ADD are often huge risk takers, quite adept at making bad decisions, and frequently make many job changes fuelled by impulsiveness.

Procrastination is a truly maddening ADD trait and causes those around them a great deal of anguish. The ADD person is most often completely unaware of the havoc their procrastination causes.

Those afflicted seem to have selective hearing when a partner tries to reason with them, and often continue on a path to potential destruction, taking their family right along with them.

Chapter 3 – The 70s
The Storm Before The Calm

As this decade began, life looked grim. Bob's job loss shortly after moving back to Connecticut was soon followed by a bike accident. One early spring day, after Bob repaired one of our kids' bicycles, he took it for a test ride. Riding down a steep hill, he slid on sand and fell onto the pavement. He needed major facial plastic surgery to repair the damage.

Adding to our problems was the fact that he had not been able to collect unemployment insurance, since his last position had been as an independent contractor—commission only. The accident and recuperation time meant he was unable to job hunt for many weeks. When he finally recovered, there seemed to be no employment opportunities in our somewhat rural section of southeastern Connecticut. Our funds were quickly disappearing.

Bob took a temporary sales position for a few months, although it did not quite cover our basic needs. When that job ended, we were in serious trouble. All profits from the sale of our New Jersey home were wiped out.

Without unemployment funds or job prospects, we were about to lose our home.

Our children asked if they were going to starve to death. They were frightened, and so was I. Bob, not so much! His approach, it seemed, was to hope for a miracle while becoming totally immobilized. What, I lamented, was wrong with him?

I insisted he start looking in Massachusetts where employment was more readily available. He said he did not like Massachusetts ... bad drivers, etc. I was thinking more along the lines of eating, rather than bad drivers! I could not convince him to put aside his selfish, stubborn feelings about "location". He had a way of putting up an invisible wall and no discussion was possible. But after neighbors brought us leftover food from a community picnic (which we chose not to attend), Bob suddenly felt prompted to start that job search in Massachusetts after all. Procrastination and stubbornness frequently played a key role in our disastrous situations.

It was then that I started developing severe hives, as stress was taking a huge toll on me mentally and physically. We put our home, only a year and a half old, up for sale. Only this time we had absolutely no place to go. Bob had not found employment as yet, and we had no money left.

My dad offered to co-sign for an apartment for us if the house sold and Bob was still unemployed. He gave us money for food and a credit card for gas. I was humiliated, but not Bob. He never felt embarrassed or any of the other emotions that most people feel.

Looking back now, I realize that since he had no close friends (and he never did after his school years), he had no need to be concerned with humiliation. But at that time, I was much too immersed in basic survival issues to give much thought to that. I was baffled though. How had we managed to get to such a low point? Bob was smart enough and had great potential, but he was letting his family down on a continuous basis.

Besides being puzzled by his lack of emotion, I was now totally consumed with multiple fears: financial problems, job security, potential loss of our home, and the need to maintain a mentally stable environment for our children. I did all this worrying by myself, often feeling like a single parent. I realized that the actions needed to right our wrongs were not only "strongly suggested" by me, they had to be implemented by me as well. Bob never seemed able to recognize problems, let alone solve them. However, he sure was quite the wizard at creating them! Over the years, I sat up alone through many long nights, trying to figure out solutions to get us through whatever current mess we were in. This turned out to be good training for me. In the years ahead, as dire circumstances escalated, it became crucial that I do this often for our survival.

Then, in 1972, as we were about to lose our home, which had not sold, our luck changed. My persistence in writing cover letters for Bob to Massachusetts companies finally paid off. He was offered an excellent position as a manager of marketing communications for a cutting-edge technical company not far from the New Hampshire border. Relief!

Off he went immediately to start his new job, leaving me to carry on selling our home. With that accomplished, we bought and moved into a home in Massachusetts. I truly hated this new house, although it was in a decent enough family neighborhood, but we were now too poor to be fussy. Next up was to get the kids registered in school and start all over again.

The new position paid rather well, which was a blessing. But that job was the most stressful Bob ever had, then or since. He became cranky and was agitated all the time to the point that he needed a glass of scotch as soon as he walked in the door from work. That had never been his habit before. He wanted no children around, only me to help him calm down. He was like a time bomb ready to explode at any moment.

On top of this, I disliked our new town and was feeling extremely lonely. Even if I were willing to share my stressful predicament (and I was not), there was no one to talk with.

I was confused, yet embarrassed; my personal dignity seemed to be at stake.

It was during this year that my dad died suddenly at age 56. Shocked and devastated, I now added my mother to my worries. She had an extremely difficult time as a sudden widow.

Although I never took any pills to help with my depression, Bob began taking Valium, and life was more tolerable for our whole family. After only a short time however, I had him discontinue this tranquilizer as it was making him too lethargic. But I sure missed the peace and tranquility we enjoyed for a while.

Then, unexpectedly in 1974, good things began happening. My mother married a very nice gentleman, and Bob received a new job offer in technical sales.

Because he was so desperate to make a change from his mega stressful employment situation, he had willingly participated in this job search. I had suggested he look for a (technical) sales position this time, as I thought it would better suit his temperament. He ended up enjoying this type of work and did quite well.

Finally, I decided it was time to make peace with our location, and made a successful effort to become involved within the community.

But only a few months later, out of the blue, Bob received an unsolicited offer from a Massachusetts sales representative firm requesting that he relocate anywhere in Connecticut and handle electronic sales in that state for them. They knew Bob through business dealings in his previous marketing communications position.

I was so tired of relocating, and the thought of restructuring my life yet again was too overwhelming to contemplate. We decided to turn down this offer, but it was presented twice more, with increased salary and perks each time. Finally, I was convinced that we should accept this opportunity after all.

In the spring of 1974, we were back in Connecticut, our favorite state. We bought a home in an upscale, family-friendly, shoreline town in the New Haven area. I registered the kids in school and joined the Newcomers Club, where I developed wonderful lifelong friendships. (We lived in that town for 24 years.)

The biggest change this job offered Bob was the opportunity to work from home, a newish concept in 1974, and he loved it. However, he became a hermit of sorts in his home office, rarely leaving except for business appointments. He seldom shopped for himself; he had zero patience waiting in line to pay. I bought everything he needed.

However, much of his impatience also involved a very low tolerance for anything Scott did. This became so stressful for Ava and me, that I began finding ways to keep our son away from his dad when he came home from school. I attempted to create a peaceful respite for us at dinnertime, but that usually turned into a nightmare. For some reason, Bob seemed to hyper-focus on everything Scott did. Even minor infractions, such as making noise with his fork, were not tolerated. Unable to believe what was going on, I lived in a perpetual state of anxiety.

In early 1975, with our children ages eleven and thirteen, I accepted an almost full-time position at a local newspaper as an outside advertising sales representative. Selling and designing display advertisements suited my social and creative needs. I enjoyed friendships in the office, working with my clients out of the office, and was very happy to have a territory close to home.

A year later, I was offered the position of advertising manager for an affiliated publication, but turned it down. This was a 45-minute commute and I knew I needed to remain closer to home and my children. I was increasingly becoming more concerned about our dysfunctional family.

During this time, Scott refused to actively participate in his classes. Teachers often called me insisting that I find a way to get him to do his homework. Sometimes he would just sit in the class, they said, quietly staring into space.

At home, he had his own room, his own desk, and we offered him help, but he just seemed unable to commit to his responsibilities. His confused teachers decided to test him just to see what the problem might be. They thought he had learning disabilities. I said he was just lazy. The test results proved he had no learning disabilities and that he had a very high IQ. There was no mention of ADD.

In retrospect, I can now see the ADD pattern growing in Scott. He struggled through school, and I pegged him as lazy, but deep down I knew something was wrong.

For instance, when we lived in Massachusetts his teachers wanted him in a new experimental classroom that would require each student to work on his own, at his own pace. I insisted they not force this experiment on Scott, as it was quite apparent to me he would not survive learning independently. He always needed lots of push, nagging, and organization to get him to do anything.

I suggested there were others like him, and insisted they set up a separate class for those children who needed structure and guidelines. Fortunately they did.

During the mid and late 70s, Bob found success in his career. He had a talent for selling sophisticated electronic products to industries in Connecticut. Finally, he had an income that allowed us to feel more financially secure. This gave us a much needed respite and our lifestyle improved greatly.

Yes, Bob was still somewhat impatient, but

a happier person overall. He went out one day for a haircut and—surprise—came home with a sailboat (another example of impulsiveness)! However, he discovered a new hobby, which we as a family all enjoyed. Over the next few years, he bought two larger boats, and our weekends were spent sailing on Long Island Sound. Sailing became his passion and obsession, and he taught our kids how to sail as well. Ava and Scott were very happy and thought all this goodness would now last forever. But in spite of this, I somehow intuitively knew the truth—that this was a special time gifted to us, but one that would not last.

Although Ava and I enjoyed a very close mother-daughter relationship, she was relieved to leave our home situation behind when she began college in 1979. She spent her teen years frequently annoyed at Scott for upsetting our household dynamics. She could not understand why he didn't follow the rules. Ava got along fine with her dad. As a quick learner, she knew exactly what would set him off and was careful to avoid irritating him.

That same year we decided to build a new home about a mile away. We were well into the design stage of our dream home when Bob became very agitated again, unfairly and constantly picking on our son. There was no reasoning with him. I was so tired of the negative energy once again spreading throughout our unhappy dwelling that I demanded we get some professional help. I even began seriously thinking about leaving after all. However, Bob did agree to counseling, a huge step for him and us as a couple.

The first person we saw needed more help than we did. But we searched further and found a pleasant enough counselor. For the whole hour, Bob rambled on nonstop, but not about anything related to our problem. She had not a single clue as to how to help us. Unfortunately, she was not remotely aware of Adult ADD symptoms and neither were we. So we decided not to waste our time and moved on.

I missed my daughter so much when she went to college. I was left alone with the two dysfunctional men in my life. Ava would arrive home for visits, so happy to see us, and then as the visit deteriorated, she could not wait to get back to college.

Many years would pass before we found the expert help we needed. Meanwhile, we just continued on, unknowingly living a multifaceted ADD life. The one thing I was absolutely sure of: I was not the "crazy one"!

ADD Notes

When ADD is present in the home, *all* family members suffer. Family dynamics are often controlled by the ADD member tainting the atmosphere, sometimes ruining an entire day for everyone. Mothers may be constantly yelling to control ADD children or ADD adults may be acting grouchy, impatient, and irrational. There are a dozen different and perplexing scenarios that can and do happen daily.

Other symptoms include chronic impatience over minor or non-events and talking incessantly—sometimes in a lecturing manner—without allowing others to join in. This particular unacceptable social characteristic tends to alienate everyone in their presence.

Chapter 4 – The 80s
Let The Good Times Roll

In the early 80s we were finally feeling somewhat at peace. Indeed, there were still occasional issues, but the respite from continuous tension was a great relief. Bob's business successes kept him happy and focused. And when members of our extended family needed help, we tackled those issues together as a team.

Up to this point, life had been unusually complex, but I began to feel optimistic and pleased that Bob's new, happier self meant we could put that all behind us. Any fantasies I had before about leaving diminished during this calm and hopeful time. I felt that the "old Bob" I fell in love with was back.

However, in the recent past, while consumed with unhappy thoughts of escaping my confusing life, I pinpointed and faced some hard cold facts: if I were to leave, dividing our assets would have left both of us floundering financially. Whatever we owned was heavily mortgaged. The realistic economic downside of separating was very scary.

Then, too, even though I was working, I never made enough to support two children on my own. My heightened intuitiveness niggled at me with the distinct possibility that by leaving there might be no child support if Bob became unemployed—a common situation for him. If not pushed, prodded, and helped with resumes and cover letters, Bob would sit around for weeks doing nothing to find work. The unfortunate truth was that without my overseeing his career, he would falter. He was never able to motivate himself past procrastination or impulsiveness, especially when it came to seeking employment.

Perhaps you have to live with an ADD person to fully comprehend the necessity for an ongoing and active mentor to be physically present daily in the home. For a spouse in my position, doing otherwise was putting financial survival at serious risk.

As Bob's enabler, damage control routinely became my responsibility. That continued as our ritual and how we existed. Additionally, it was always important to me to keep our family intact even though I knew we were a bit dysfunctional. In spite of all those puzzling issues infringing on our lives, we were still surprisingly a tightly bonded family.

I sometimes wonder now what I might have done if I had been a woman-of-means: Would I have made such an effort to "tough it out"? Maybe love is not always enough. (But the answer to that remains forever unknown.)

In the fall of 1980, we moved into our

newly built country contemporary home, nestled in two beautiful wooded acres, near our former residence. After much stress dealing with assorted construction problems, we happily settled in. Bob had a spacious new home office and I was still working for the newspaper. Ava was in college and Scott was a high school senior. Although he and Bob were still functioning as an oil and water combo, I kept imagining how calm it would soon be when our son left for college.

From the mid-70s to the mid-80s we enjoyed a financially secure life. During that time Bob was, like many middle class Americans, working hard and reaping the rewards of an incredible economy. Suddenly we were comfortable enough to build that custom "home of our dreams," purchase an apartment house as an investment, and enjoy sailing our boat on Long Island Sound.

Wow ... what an exhilarating change from the 60s and early 70s.

Scott graduated from high school in 1981. His school years had been very difficult for him and me. Homework and tests were always an issue, but he managed to get into a state college. However, at the end of his first year he was put on academic probation. Bob and I opted not to waste money to send him back for another year of "partying." Since we knew he had a high IQ, we naturally assumed he was too lazy to do what was necessary to maintain decent grades. We offered him two choices: either join the military or get a job and move out on his own. The tension in our home, with him there, was too much for me to consider anything else. Both he and Bob were constantly disappointing each other with their assorted and unrecognized ADD symptoms. I thought we all needed a break.

Scott chose the army, as I knew he would, and for two years was stationed in Panama in the Military Police Corp. He did fine in the service, as the structured life kept him focused. When he returned, he reenrolled in college but continued to seriously struggle. I suggested he leave and simply try to make his way through life without a degree. While it appeared that college was not a good fit for him, this suggestion seemed to challenge him in a positive way, and he finally did graduate. Years later, of course, when we realized the reason everything was so difficult for him, we sympathized, and Bob apologized for constantly criticizing him.

Towards the mid-80s, Bob was still successfully working for the sales firm that recruited him in 1974. Then suddenly they asked him to train a new younger man because (they said) the territory was growing. They gave this young man a salary and a company car, and left him with Bob to be coached.

While Bob looked at this only as an inconvenience, I saw it as the beginning of the end! It was obvious to me that Bob was being pushed aside to make way for a younger person who had a contract that would prevent him from receiving the high income Bob earning.

Most savvy people know situations like this occur in business. But Bob seemed to think this would not happen to him. I thought that strange, since I clearly envisioned him being dismissed as soon as he finished grooming his charge. Unfortunately, that is exactly what happened.

Bob felt training this new rep was the right thing to do, simply because it was requested of him. I love the fact that our generation has such honorable work ethics and likes to do the right thing. I did not, however, think this was the right or necessary thing for him to do, but I could not convince him of that. Neither could he wrap his head around the fact that he needed to seek other employment immediately, whether he was willing to help someone else or not. After all, we had a large mortgage along with other heavy financial commitments.

Not surprisingly, Bob was quite shocked and disappointed when he was let go. Since unemployment insurance is not available to independent contractors, we did not have a financial safety net. All during this time, while Bob was demonstrating complete unawareness and denial, I felt bewildered, frustrated, angry ... and powerless.

Unfortunately, a large chunk of earned

commission owed to Bob was withheld by this firm when he was dismissed. He hired an attorney, but ended up settling, resulting in the loss of much of those funds.

Now stressed, both financially and emotionally, and with no new employment on the horizon, Bob spent the next four months moping around the house with no idea of what he wanted to do next. Once again we, or I should say *I*, carefully went through newspapers for opportunities—no online job posting in those days. He occasionally called a head-hunter but did little else.

My anger grew with each wasted day. Yet again, he was simply not reacting appropriately to the severe financial mess we were in. I could not engage his brain to participate in solving this problem. He tended to thrive best in rote situations, which this was clearly not.

Another sad and complicated family matter unexpectedly appeared right in the middle of all this ongoing chaos. My dear mother was diagnosed as terminally ill with leukemia. So while grappling with Bob's unemployment and Scott's army and college stresses, I was additionally confronted with the dilemma of how best to care for my mother who lived in Florida.

I quickly became a reluctant member of the "sandwich" generation. I felt the weight of the world squarely on my shoulders. Relatives insisted I move in with my mother until she passed, but I could not leave my unemployed husband, who was in desperate need of both prodding and support. Nor could I afford to leave or lose my job, which had become our only income. Of course, I never shared these concerns with those family members. I did not want any of this to get back to my mother and make her last days a time of worry. She had always been so supportive over the years, but I could not involve her this time, not in her condition.

To my mother's credit, she never asked me to move in with her. Perhaps she just somehow sensed my plight. She did have a doting husband, although he was not able to be all that she needed during her illness. However, I am so appreciative that family members living in Florida were kind, loving, and supportive to her. Eventually I did fly out to be with my mother near the end.

I returned home after she passed, sad and depressed, only to find my husband still unsure about what to do next to make a living. My job at the newspaper, thankfully, was still intact. Since I was responsible for about one third of the paper's revenues, I knew they would have had no choice but to replace me had I left for an unknown extended time period.

Meanwhile, our meager funds were quickly disappearing. That left me only one alternative. I suggested to Bob that he start his own electronic sales representative firm.

He really thrived in that career before, so why not? Nothing else positive was happening. Our financial situation was becoming dire, and with only my modest income, there was no way to take care of all our expenses.

Bob jumped at this idea and his new rep business was launched. The downside of this meant that Bob would reap only a very small income for about two years as he worked to establish his new company. This was a very risky venture to tackle financially, but our choices were so limited.

We tightened our belts even more and forged ahead. After a couple of years of struggling to remain solvent, business started to gel. We were recouping and successfully moving forward. That afforded me an opportunity to soon start a new venture myself.

Looking to make a change from my newspaper job, I accepted an interesting position with a statewide nanny placement agency. I really enjoyed the new challenges while learning about this service, which placed legal (American) nannies from around the country into private homes. The agency owner assigned me a local territory, and as soon as I became licensed I worked from my home office.

About six months later, the owner told me she was moving to California and insisted I buy my limited territory as a franchise. That was definitely not to my liking. Because she could not legally prevent me from doing so, I established my own nanny placement agency in 1986.

I had no limitations on territory anymore. The entire country was mine. I worked long hours for the next several years and loved it. Bob, always my best cheerleader, was willing to lend a hand and support me in this—or any venture I chose to become involved with.

I eventually sold that agency in 1993 to a very capable woman. After training her, she willingly embraced the high standards and ethics of the company. I then moved on and used my business skills in new ways.

In spite of some major problems in the 80s, this was a fruitful decade. Ava married a wonderful man in 1987, and we felt rather peaceful and relaxed for the next couple of years, just Bob and me in our empty nest. But, sadly, this was not to last ....

ADD Notes

If by some miracle there was just one ADD characteristic I could eliminate, it would be the total lack of awareness so common to this disorder. There are many characteristics of ADD and different degrees of severity, too, but for so many, life events are severely impacted by this particular major symptom.

As is often the case with ADD people, Bob's offensive actions were never deliberate; quite the contrary. He was completely oblivious and unaware of his offensive behavior. He had no idea how damaging the effects of his actions were on others either.

ADD unawareness is frequently the culprit involved with procrastination, impulsivity, social faux pas, etc. Understandably, this causes much confusion to those around them. This handicap is likely to create much havoc in business situations as well.

Chapter 5 – The 90s
The Good, the Bad, and the Ugly

Part 1

This decade began well with a lucky breakthrough for us. Finally, we had a diagnosis for our son: ADD. It changed his life and the lives of those that loved him, too.

Scott was struggling in all ways possible. Soon after he graduated college, job changes became a constant. Shortly after he began his first job, his employer advised him to look for another position. He said Scott was not suited for the type of work he had been hired to do. But since the employer liked him, he gave Scott time to apply elsewhere while still employed. To my way of thinking, this was a gift. However, our son did not believe he would be dismissed. "He likes me. He won't let me go," he said. So when he was dismissed a couple of months later, Scott was shocked.

After that there was a succession of quick jobs, one after another. Some lasted months, some only a few weeks. I grew more worried with each change. What was wrong with our intelligent and very likable son? Even more unsettling was the thought of what might eventually happen to him.

Although we helped Scott, his discomfort at having to accept food and clothing from his parents created an edgy relationship with the three of us for a short time. I understood this, but still, he needed the help. Although he was living on his own, he was almost thirty and single, and I was fearful for his future. I helped him gain employment with a former employer of mine, and then just held my breath hoping he would perform well.

I am not a big TV watcher. When it is on, I am usually doing something else and only half listening. However, one evening the popular show *20/20* happened to be on. The segment concerned a young boy of about twelve who had ADD. (After this boy had been diagnosed, his father thought that he himself might have ADD, too.) Suddenly my focus was 100% on the television set. Symptoms familiar to me were being rattled off, along with the problems they caused. They discussed solutions as well.

Imagine all this information on one lone TV show! I was giddy with happiness. Someone was describing my son's exact situations. I grabbed a pen and wrote down the name of the book they were discussing that was soon to change Scott's life—*Driven to Distraction* by Dr. Edward Hallowell.

The next day I raced to the store to buy this encouraging narrative. I enjoy reading very much, but had never before done speed reading. I zipped through this hardcover in one day, and my joy was incredible. I found the reason (and a "cure") for what was ruining Scott's life. I immediately called and told him that I now knew what his lifelong problem was ... and how to fix it! Scott was confused by my excitement, but agreed to listen and cooperate.

My first step was to find a psychologist who would diagnose him. That was not easy in those days, but I was persistent. The next step was to carefully prepare notes for that important two hour initial appointment. I did that by describing my son's thirty-year history, thus explaining why I thought he had ADD. (I knew that would be the first question asked of me.)

Since I did not want to use up an excessive amount of time, I spoke quickly using notes to spill out three decades of Scott's struggles through school and issues in his current life. I detailed his inappropriate responses to situations and his odd thinking process by offering examples. Then I went into the waiting room. I had done my job by introducing Scott to a whole new world of understanding. Two more visits and many tests later (with me not in attendance), it was official: he had definite and unrelenting ADD.

Now that we had a diagnosis, I felt powerful and was able to focus on a solution. Then, the most amazing thing happened. Bob, who had always picked on his son for just about everything, told him all was forgiven! He told Scott he realized he had a "condition not in his control" and nothing he had done was his fault after all. It seemed to foster a new understanding and caring relationship between them. In spite of this, I know our son carries permanent scars from a lifetime of not fulfilling his father's expectations.

Since psychologists cannot prescribe medications, we needed to find a physician who understood this condition—not just in children, but in adults as well. Ritalin® was prescribed and quickly became a favorite household word.

Listening to my son describe his first day on Ritalin was exhilarating. He said he felt like an octopus that could do ten things at once with ease, clarity, and pleasure. By some sort of miracle, and with the help of a television show and a book on ADD, I felt like I had given birth again to a much happier, more grounded and productive son.

Life continued on well for him for many years. He was doing things that seemed impossible in his past, but now anything was possible. Soon after his diagnosis, he married a lovely young woman, whom we happily welcomed into our family. She knew about his condition, which was thankfully well controlled with Ritalin. I suggested to her that life might still be a bit difficult, but I felt that this remarkable medication would allow those afflicted to enjoy a normal life. How naïve and unrealistic I was.

Notice that in the midst of all this enthusiasm I never mentioned Bob's issues. In fact, it did cross all our minds that maybe Bob had ADD, too. But Bob, ever the optimist, felt that was not possible. After all, he had always been an excellent student, and unlike his son, really liked school. With no academic issues in his past, he was completely confident he was not afflicted. We never seemed to go to the next step: talking with a professional about his personality flaws and major problems. Knowing little about an ADD genetic connection, we focused instead on helping our son. I was just getting acquainted with what having ADD really meant. More in depth knowledge would come later though, precipitated by ruinous events.

By the beginning of this decade, I realized that I had long ago, and quite subconsciously, developed a coping strategy that helped me maintain my sanity. I had cleverly created an imaginary Pandora's Box that housed my confusion, hurts, anger, and tangible life grievances, all of which had a huge impact on my precarious emotions. With several locks to keep the box tightly shut, it worked very well. By dumping all my sorrows into this container, I could forgive Bob and function well enough most of the time. Notice that I did not say "I forgot." I have never forgotten a single incident. I just put them away.

Those past issues came back to haunt me

sometimes, but mostly when a new major problem erupted. Then the locks broke, and up flew the lid! All the miseries of the past were flung in my face again. Bob then accused me of bringing up dated unpleasant events. An argument invariably ensued. I always seemed to be stuffing the old wounds back into the box and frequently adding new ones. However, it was, and still is a rather useful tool for coping.

Part 2

Happy as we were to have finally solved a problem that had plagued our son for many years, it was tempting to go back to the "what ifs". What if the school testing had revealed his condition years before? What if, what if? But, as we observed the many positive changes happening in our son's life, we decided to move on.

The early 90s were an interesting time for me. After selling my nanny agency, I became a contributing columnist for an industry newsletter. I also wrote instructive newspaper articles with thoughts of encouraging publishers to consider a potential book about my amazing and shocking experiences as a nanny placement counselor. Eventually there was a book offer.

During this same time frame I acted as a national consultant for nanny placement firms. I guided grateful new owners to success and was an experienced resource for floundering businesses looking to remain solvent.

A couple of years later, in the mid-90s, I moved on and created a company that published specialty folders for realtors. Excited for me about this new advertising venture, Bob was very helpful, and worked with me to get started. Soon I was publishing customized folders for real estate agencies for their clients' use. (This was a lucrative business until 2001 when the real estate trade became computerized.)

Our dual home-office arrangement worked well. Bob and I shared supplies and equipment, but conducted business from totally separate work areas. We usually met in the kitchen for lunch.

During those busy years, I took Wednesdays off for bridge games and outings with friends. We considered ourselves, as women often do, a unified support system for each other, and joked that this worked as well or better than professional therapy. Whatever we discussed on our special day was respected and never shared with others. Though I enjoyed fun times with my friends, I didn't know how important their support was soon to become.

Part 3

Toward the middle of the decade, Bob

began to notice a slowdown in his business, which had been successful for several years. This was troubling to both of us. By early 1996, as the slowdown grew worse, I became extremely anxious. Suddenly Bob was paying just the minimums due on credit cards and saying things like "credit card companies usually negotiate with customers if they get into trouble."

I found this unnerving and panic was setting in. We had always paid our credit cards in full each month. Even with problems during our difficult financial past, we never borrowed from our credit cards. We were experts in thrift during tough times. But Bob and I both had business expenses now, as well as a large mortgage and other major financial commitments.

As a manufacturers' representative, Bob sold for and dealt with many different companies and personalities. From time to time, there were changes made for a variety of reasons. Companies he represented would sever relationships with him, or he would drop them, depending on the productivity or economy at the time.

As the year progressed, I became concerned that this was the beginning of the demise of Bob's company. The economy was not strong and he was not being paid promptly anymore, which was unusual. He was also dropped by a couple of firms he had represented for a long time.

I had always wondered and worried how he handled sales situations. After all, in social settings he interrupted and talked incessantly to anyone around. I had no way of knowing if this or any of his other negative traits carried over into business as well, but the hints were there.

He was not easy on people who disagreed with his way of thinking. He never seemed to realize that people did not enjoy his interrogative style of conversation. I often worried about whom he might be offending and was frustrated by his poor social behavior. Although it was not intentional, he frequently offended my friends. He rarely socialized on his own. By choice, his office was his haven. So what was going on now? Perhaps, I thought, the “rep” industry was changing after all, as had been rumored. Nevertheless, I knew it was time to create a “Plan B.”

I mistakenly thought Bob would be panicked by now as well and agree about that Plan B. But, no; that was not the case at all. He loved having his own sales firm and would not consider making any changes. In fact, he said he was expecting several potential sales orders to close at any moment and felt all would soon be straightened out financially. He said if they did not come to fruition, we could then talk about what changes to consider. With great apprehension, I agreed.

Well, guess what: those sales did not come

in. There we were, talking again a couple of weeks later. I was sure we would now move on to a Plan B. I insisted it was already past prime time to either get a job locally or make a move elsewhere, wherever he could find work. The status quo was no longer an option.

Bob, however, would not budge! He said more sales orders were still pending, but we would talk again if they did not materialize.

I protested loudly, begging for realistic reasoning from him, but he put up his hands and said there was to be no discussion on this for six months when all would be fine again. He stormed out of the room. End of conversation.

Even now, I cannot adequately express how frightened, lonely, and empty I felt. I saw tragedy ahead and he saw success! There was such a dark energy in our home. Bob was living in some sort of a fantasy world—and in total denial as well. With his steadfast and stubborn refusal to talk about this oncoming disaster, I was trapped. I felt we were headed toward certain poverty and there was nothing I could do to convince him of that.

It crossed my mind, briefly, that leaving might be the only way out of this potential disaster, at least for me. But of course, that was ridiculous. All debts were in my name, too. I had little funds for survival, and this was clearly not the right time to make such a bold decision. Now my feelings were further reinforced—although money may not buy happiness, it definitely provides options ... and I had no options!

Bob called the credit card companies to see if he could negotiate away some of his debt. Of course, he couldn't. What was he thinking? Soon after, he ran out of credit to pay the bills, and asked me for one of three credit cards listed in my name only. We were in kind of an emergency situation, he said, but would be back on track with the potential orders he was expecting shortly. Because I was terrified about our current pile of bills, I cringed and grudgingly gave him one card with no charges on it and a high credit limit. He then looked relieved instead of crazed. That just left me more terrified.

Although the immediate bills were paid, no sales came to fruition, and a couple of months later he took another of my cards to pay more bills. This time he was like a madman asking, and I was literally on the verge of a nervous breakdown. This is not a situation you readily share with neighbors and friends. My mother had been very sympathetic during our earlier times of crises, but she was gone now. I was feeling pure panic every minute of every day!

Fortunately, I had our caring and supportive adult children to commiserate with. But the three of us were befuddled as to how to rein in Bob's misguided thinking and erratic behavior.

In reality, what was happening was a total ADD breakdown of someone who was undiagnosed and in desperate need of drug therapy and counseling. But we simply did not know that then.

When ADD children have tantrums, they are sent to a time-out corner, but when ADD adults have a tantrum, which is what this was, they are capable of putting their families in grave danger. In this case, a huge financial crisis was about to erupt.

Bob asked me for my third and last credit card in early 1997. My simple reply was "over my dead body." His response: "Then we have to declare bankruptcy!"

Part 4

I was certainly not surprised by then to hear the word bankruptcy. I was angry and horrified, but not surprised. In fact, I knew it was inevitable and was just waiting for Bob to catch up and grasp that fact. I had not been able to have a meaningful conversation with him for many months.

He was numb and immobilized now, which was usually the case when a crisis occurred, even if he was responsible for it. Although I did not create this mess, I knew for sure it was going to be mine to clean up. Little did we know it was the ADD devil run amuck. I was the victim, and survival, quite literally, became my only goal.

With Bob too mentally incapacitated to help with this disaster, I knew I must remain razor sharp. I began the unpleasant task of finding the best bankruptcy lawyer. I chose three to consult with.

The first attorney was just okay. The second one really upset me. During our discussion, he said he doubted we could keep our retirement funds, which, since we were self-employed, were self-funded during our more prosperous time. I was pretty sure this was not true, but he insisted he would have to check that out.

I went home and experienced a total meltdown based on his frightening words; I no longer had a desire to live. If our small Keogh and IRA retirement funds were taken, we would probably become wards of the state. Bob had no income and I suspected our home mortgage was upside down. All this was more than I could wrap my head around. I desperately asked Bob what his plan might be to get us out of this nightmare. His reply was, “I have no idea.” He was in a state of shock.

Thankfully, that second lawyer turned out to be wrong, but by the time he came back with that information, (several long days later) I was in a severe depression. Our daughter called Bob and told him not to let me out of his sight for a single minute. She has since told me how helpless she felt, living two hours away.

I had not realized she called Bob until I noticed him following me at a discreet distance when I took long walks by the river near our home. Our children were very worried and especially concerned that I was contemplating suicide. I knew, even then, that I would never have done such a thing. However, at that time, I would sincerely not have minded dying.

After allowing myself a few more days of anger and despair, I realized I had to pull myself together to address the serious business at hand. Bob looked at me with relief and said, “I’m so glad you’re back. I’ve been waiting for your depression to pass so you could figure out how to repair this mess!”

“Bob Breaks/Linda Fixes”: our usual funky dance routine.

We finally chose lawyer number three. He told us we would lose almost everything, but not our retirement funds. Whew! We would be allowed to keep only a minimal amount of personal stocks (not in retirement funds) and bonds, but the rest would be taken to pay creditors. That meant many thousands of precious dollars would be lost to us. He also told us we could remain in our home as long as we continued paying the mortgage, which for the time being we planned to do, but it was technically included in the bankruptcy. We could keep only one car unless the second one was of little value. We lucked out on that and were able to keep both cars.

I was suddenly getting educated on a subject that I never thought I would need to know about … ever. I was so humiliated. Bob, however, was not. Since our huge credit card obligations were going to be dismissed, he seemed mostly relieved.

I remember clearly the lawyer's first words to Bob when he looked over our enormous debt: "Good God, man, what were you thinking?" Finally, someone had posed the exact question to Bob that I had been desperately trying to ask him for several months. Bob, however, had no answer.

Before this nightmare got into full swing, the lawyer told us we had to plan this out carefully. We had to stop any type of credit card payments or activity and do no unusual banking for three months. It was so stressful waiting for these months to pass while the creditors called us day and night. We were not allowed to give out any information in order to protect ourselves. We simply stopped answering the phone.

Even now as I write, I still feel physically the intense mental pain of this fiasco and the extreme hostility and anger I felt towards Bob for allowing this to happen to us. The very few who knew about this tried to assure me that it was not intentional on his part. Perhaps not intentional, but, nevertheless, it happened! I was past the end of my rope. But I knew I could not give up; though there was no name for it—that we knew of at the time—I knew that Bob was a very sick man.

While all this was going on, I knew I would eventually have to cope with social issues regarding this embarrassing situation. After all, I had many friends and was well known within our community. Shortly after we knew a bankruptcy was imminent, and while feeling quite distressed, I reluctantly went to a friend's home one evening to play bridge. It was the scheduled monthly night game with my "Wednesday Club" girlfriends.

I had been trying to appear normal for so long that they knew nothing of any of this until I broke down that night. Those girls were wonderful ... and discreet; not sharing this "gossip" with others. I felt their empathy, as they were always there for me to lean on. I will never forget their compassion and remain grateful to each one of them to this day.

The incident that was more like a swift kick in the stomach took place at our doctor's office. I went only to inquire about helpful medications for my depressed state. (I do not like to take drugs unless absolutely necessary.) I reluctantly shared our situation with him. He said he could give me medication that would work, or I could just wait out what he called "reactive depression". His next words were, "I guess it's not a crime to be stupid!" So that was my first (but not last) public introduction to feeling like a second class citizen—from my doctor no less!

Since a bankruptcy remains on all public records for ten years, I knew we were heading into a long and painful period in our life. I accepted the sample pills the doctor gave me, but threw them out when I got home. I felt I needed to be very alert for the many responsibilities ahead.

The last minute things I did before we filed were stress driven, but financially worthwhile. I asked the lawyer if I could withdraw stock (that was in my name only), valued over the allowed limit, and use that money for ongoing bills that we still had to pay anyhow, like mortgage, utilities, insurances, etc., before we filed. He said I could because all funds still belonged to me until filing. One wonders why he initially told me I would lose all that stock and not advise me of other options. I was left to figure out so much on my own.

That allowed barely seventy-two hours to get the stock released, sold, and the bills paid with those funds; so we would not have that money in our possession on filing day. My mind and body were fueled by pure adrenaline at that point. Meanwhile, desperate to leave no stone unturned, I somehow managed to get our mortgage refinanced in the nick of time, lowering the payments significantly just before our credit rating officially dropped from A to D. It helped some, for the short time we remained in that home.

Many with little knowledge of this disorder have asked me in recent years what someone with ADD might do that could be "SO terrible"! This bankruptcy is a perfect example of how dangerous a situation can become, not only for the ADD person, but for the family as well.

Until now I have not shared this mortification with anyone; I couldn't admit our downfall to others. Only our children and the few close friends who so willingly supported me knew any of this.

ADD adults routinely engage in impulsive and risky behavior. Outlandish decisions can be a part of any scenario in their daily lives. Financial ruin, so common to ADD people, is a distinct possibility and obviously one of the most damaging. Their thinking is often irrational and, even worse, they can lose touch with reality and become unreachable.

One pattern I continuously noticed (and have since read about) is that people with ADD constantly repeat mistakes, making the same gaffes over and over as if they never happened before. They seem to learn nothing from their past. If you re-read some of the earlier chapters you will realize, as I do, that this tragedy was no doubt an accident waiting to happen.

We filed our bankruptcy papers in September 1997, sitting in a courtroom surrounded by other sad souls doing the same. The official discharge of our debt was finalized in December 1997. We had to start all over again, at ages sixty and fifty-five, with only our small retirement fund to sustain us. But Bob had no job. We had an upside down mortgage and a very poor credit score after thirty-five years of A-plus. What a challenge surviving this was going to be! I was unsure how I was going to handle this latest and most humiliating experience. Extremely frightened, I wondered if we would endure after this financial tragedy.

Part 5

Somehow, 1998 turned out to be an amazing year for us. Fresh in the throes of newfound poverty, I needed to formulate a brand new life plan. Bob was having no luck securing employment. Connecticut and New England in general were too expensive for us to remain living there. We also knew we would realize not a single penny from selling the home we had owned for the last eighteen years. What a mess!

In our current circumstances, Bob was technically already retired, albeit not voluntarily. I knew we needed to move to a less expensive and perhaps warmer area. Bob could look for employment there—wherever "there" was to be. I still had my small real estate publishing business, which I could work from anywhere.

We put our home up for sale, but since the bank would not consider accepting a "short sale", that was a waste of time. We certainly could not come up the many thousands we would need to add to the sale proceeds to pay off the mortgage. Since the house was previously included as part of the bankruptcy, it was not necessary to have a foreclosure. The house was ours to keep only if we continued paying the still hefty mortgage on it. I truly grieved. The loss of the home that I loved caused me much distress, sadness, and additional humiliation—if that were possible.

By chance, I found an advertisement for an adult community in Central Florida that sounded spectacular. It was reasonably priced, especially by Connecticut standards, and the warm climate was very enticing. The only negative was that we did not especially like Florida. My mother had lived in south Florida in her last years, but it never appealed to us. We often said we would never move to Florida ... never say never.

I did not tell Bob that I had sent for the literature and video. When it arrived, he was unimpressed because it was a Florida location, but we decided we would watch the tape anyhow and then just toss it. But we watched in awe and then showed it to our kids.

A couple of weeks later, on a cold winter day in March, we flew to Florida to check out this flourishing locale. We ended our short stay by placing a deposit on a small but perfect three bedroom, two-bath, two-car-garage home that would be built and ready for us to move into in August. This cheered me up a lot. I felt hopeful once again.

Back in Connecticut, I began preparing to

move out of our ten-room residence. I told Bob I would handle the garage sales, clearing out eighteen years of clutter, and working with dealers to sell the big pieces that would not fit in our new, smaller home. We had a giant dumpster brought to our yard and filled it twice. I interviewed several movers and found a small private company that charged about half the price of the major moving firms. For several weeks before the move, every day was consumed with packing and making calls to cancel utilities, etc., as well as arranging for new services in Florida.

I assigned Bob just ONE thing to take charge of: to do his best to try to secure a mortgage. We knew that with our now bad credit, it would be a challenge, and the interest rate would be sky high, too. Bob found a broker who was "sure" it would not be a problem. He later stalled, giving only a probable okay. But he did say at one point it would be better if we would agree to say we would be renting out our Connecticut home, instead of giving it back to the bank. However, that would have been a lie, and we quickly rejected his suggestion. He then implied to Bob that he was still hopeful. Frankly, I was much too overwhelmed with everything I was doing to get involved with Bob's *one* assignment. That *he* was not more involved with his only responsibility, however, became an issue.

With the moving van filled and tears

flowing, we left New England—and our children, grandchildren, and friends—in August. Off we drove to Florida. But, Bob still did not have a definite answer about a mortgage for the home we were closing on in three days! I was plagued with so many other tasks that I foolishly had encouraged and expected this sixty-year-old man to handle this one obligation. Silly me; I really should have known better!

During this trip I insisted several times that Bob contact the broker who did not have our car cell phone number. (We did not have personal cell phones yet.) Bob stubbornly insisted it was not "his problem" and that it surely would be all settled (or not) automatically, between the mortgage broker and closing agent when we arrived.

Because of my real concern—not getting a mortgage at all—I was astute enough to bring cash with us to Florida to pay for the house in case it was not approved. I was able to temporarily borrow the money for this through our son's large credit lines. If our mortgage request was turned down, the plan was to try locally to get a mortgage after we moved in using our retirement funds only as a very last resort.

About twelve hours before the closing, we checked into a hotel in our new community still not knowing if the mortgage had been approved. At that time I demanded that Bob "make that damn call already!" That was how and when we found out we did not qualify.

I was beyond livid, not because of this unsuccessful outcome, that I expected, but at Bob's lax attitude. It was at that point that I tearfully told him, if he did not agree to get psychological help, our marriage was doomed. I was "so done". He had been completely inept for so long that I knew something dreadful had to be wrong with him. Not only was he continually landing in the "gutter of life", he was dragging me down with him every time. I could only think, *is this what you do to someone you love?* This was truly a double whammy because I was desperately trying to survive; to rise from the ashes and start all over again.

I knew that if not for my initiative and willingness to seek out less expensive areas of the country, as well as my fierce overall determination to carry on, we would have ended up living in government housing ... or worse.

Bob agreed that after we got settled he would seriously seek help. After episodes like this, when his mind seemed to regenerate itself, he often felt badly that he had again let me down. But still, he never seemed to comprehend how destructive his actions were or the grief they caused me. For many years after this life-changing catastrophe, I felt diminished as a person and no longer like the upstanding individual I had been.

Part 6

After settling in our newly built Florida home, I was cautiously hopeful for the first time in a very long time. After all, who would have thought such a thing was even possible just a few months before? It had taken a monumental effort to get to this wonderful place, and I felt so deserving of this reprieve.

We found it easy to make friends quickly in our new community. To my surprise, Bob became socially outgoing, although his social skills were still sometimes primitive. He liked everything about this significant change in our life. He took up tennis for the first time and loved it. This was the best outcome that could have happened to us, coming from such dire circumstances.

I brought my small publishing business with me and was successfully working part-time at home. I spent my free time playing tennis, Mah Jongg, and forming a book club. My old optimistic self was steadily returning.

During our first year in Florida, we had many important things to accomplish, too. We needed to get a mortgage in our own name. It was imperative that we do this to start rebuilding our credit rating. It took me a while to convince Bob this was the right thing to do. It just seemed easier to him to pay the ridiculously high interest rate to our son's credit cards. But I insisted on the mortgage and quickly secured one, albeit with a high interest rate. This could not be helped. We needed not only to rebuild our credit, but restore our son's credit lines back to him. I knew, over the years as our credit rating improved, we would be refinancing again.

My mental and emotional health had taken a severe beating. I was married, but without a contributing partner. Something had to be done about that.

When we attempted to address Bob's mental health issue, we discovered that few psychiatric facilities were in existence in our new area. However, we made an appointment with a small office that was part of a larger Florida based center. We had little guidance in trying to explain Bob's issues to our assigned psychologist.

She was uncomfortable because she obviously did not know how to help us. Unable to understand or address our situation, she instead tended to grasp onto something insignificant Bob mentioned and babble on about it just to fill the hour.

We still were not ADD savvy, but it was 1999, and we now firmly believe that she, as a professional, should have been aware of his symptoms as being indicative of Adult ADD. After a couple of appointments, we both were very discouraged and disappointed. It made no sense to continue and we just gave up on ever finding help. This was a real downer.

Meanwhile, Bob was enjoying fun in the sun, which was becoming a serious issue with me. He was supposed to be looking for a job after we settled in. But no, he had decided he had worked enough in his life and was not going to seek employment anymore. No way was I buying into that, especially after what he put us through!

Thus began a succession of what I called "stupid jobs." He accepted work that required only that he be breathing to be hired. None of those commission sales jobs ever paid a thing. He went from one to another. His judgment proved ridiculous.

One in particular stands out as the scariest. He was to sell a "big ticket" furniture item via in-home demonstration by appointments. The training lasted a week, and immediately after he was out in the field expecting to make sales. The manufacturer set up the appointments, sending him all over Central Florida, sometimes two or more hours away from home.

They would give him three appointments a day, six days a week, instead of the five days originally promised. This often required working from 8:00 am until 10:00 pm or later, mostly because of the long distances he was traveling. Since his normal bedtime was 10:00 pm, I worried that he would fall asleep at the wheel while driving. Additionally, people were often not at home when he arrived for these so called pre-arranged appointments, and company policy did not allow for him to call ahead to confirm.

I felt this outlandish job was a huge mistake financially and otherwise, especially since he had to pay his own expenses. It posed a danger to his health as well with the high stress and excessively long hours.

But he refused to leave this nonproductive situation, even after three weeks of this nonsense. Again, Bob was in a "stuck mode" and denial, not realizing what an absurd "career" this turned out to be! Worse yet, he became somewhat crazed, saying he just needed to get "up to speed" to be successful.

Even though he was taking his blood pressure medicine, I could see his eyes bulging. No doubt his hypertension was dangerously high. He was overwhelmed and agitated all the time. He ate poorly, was never home for dinner, barely slept, and in fact was coming unglued. Still he flat-out refused to talk to me about what was happening, and he never made a sale either.

My panic began to rise. I expected him to have a heart attack at any moment. I did not know how to extricate my husband from this extremely intense situation, thinking it would surely kill him if he continued. He was hyper-focusing on this job and again became out of touch with reality! It reminded me of his persistence when he would not close down his failing business in Connecticut. Another example of lessons not learned and mistakes repeated.

Out of desperation, I brainstormed. In the

middle of the night, I wrote him a long letter telling him how concerned I was for his health and safety. I said that we would survive, or not, but not with this job which was killing him ... literally. It was obvious he was a complete energetic mess.

Frightened, I left my letter on the counter where he ate breakfast before leaving to begin his twelve-hour day; I am a night owl and sleep late into the morning. When I awoke, he was still home and announced that he had read my letter and immediately called the company to quit. The letter totally defused him, as I hoped it might, in a way that arguing and screaming could not.

There was not to be any worthwhile employment for Bob before the turn of the century. This caused me a continuing sense of financial insecurity and my desperate feelings grew. We decided to seek help once again for Bob's baffling mental issues. That turned out to be a major two-year undertaking, with twists, turns, and even an unsettling and dangerous misdiagnosis.

Although I love my husband, I clearly did not like him very much during this sad and revolting decade.

ADD Notes

ADD symptoms vary! Be aware that everyone afflicted does not have the same difficulties. Just because one does not exhibit some of the better known characteristics, such as poor school performance, inability to organize, constant tardiness, and projects left unfinished, they still may have ADD. More subtle indications may be apparent, such as unawareness, agitation, procrastination, incessant talking, and poor decision making.

Often, in spite of situations recognized by a spouse (or friend) as perilous, no amount of warning, pleading, or discussion seems to prevent these impaired persons from continuing on the path to disaster. Much like a runaway train, their actions become unstoppable. These self-centered acts can result in compromising the family finances, trust, and stability.

One of the most painful truths to comprehend (and be prepared for) is that mistakes *will* be repeated. ADD folks do not learn from them, as most others do, and repeat the very same blunders over and over. Not surprisingly, the divorce rate in ADD marriages is incredibly high.

Chapter 6 – 2000-2010
In Sickness and in Health

Part 1

Much of this decade was dedicated to repairing mind and body. It was about "all things medical", totally consuming and sometimes life threatening. We began the century committed to the arduous task of getting Bob diagnosed with whatever had caused us such grief over the last forty years. In spite of what we now knew about ADD, Bob still felt his problem was not an ADD issue.

Then, suddenly, his total unawareness and denial about a serious physical health concern created the urgency to pursue this matter quickly after all.

He began losing weight rapidly. He had been quite thin all his life, but now he was becoming gaunt, and in a very short time. Most people would suspect that they had a problem if they had not changed their eating habits. Many women might initially be elated, but then wisely concerned. I was very worried because Bob literally seemed to be wasting away and he was totally unaware of this development.

Our friends and neighbors kept asking me what was wrong with him. They thought he was ill, and he surely looked it. But Bob did not realize he had lost weight. He told me that it was probably tennis related that he looked “so trim”. I was not buying into that. I begged him to look in the mirror and see what everyone else saw, but he refused. I managed to convince him to “just get on the damn scale already”. He was really shocked when he realized he had indeed lost fifteen pounds! That old awareness problem, which had been the cause of many major issues over the years, had now become hazardous to his physical health.

When a trip to his primary doctor showed an elevated glucose level, I thought we were on our way to a diagnosis and help. But no, the doctor didn’t think it was a big deal, maybe just something to watch. So, Bob said, “See? I’m fine,” and told me to stop worrying. I paid no attention to that comment and scheduled an appointment with an endocrinologist. This physician said Bob’s glucose number was in the diabetic range, but sent him home advising him to eat more fruits and vegetables! No medications, no diet, just more veggies. Since we have always been advocates of a healthy diet we were already enjoying copious amounts of fruits and vegetables—nothing new meant no hope for improvement!

More research and questioning of friends

and neighbors led us to an excellent endocrinologist, although it was an hour away. She successfully got Bob on track with his diabetes problem, and he accepted a new style of eating along with several medications. This discovery took much more than normal diligence on my part. I had been fighting someone in total denial for months. On his own, Bob would not have realized what grave physical danger he was in until it was too late.

With more urgency now, my next mission was to locate a psychiatrist to evaluate his mental situation. We found one close by who turned out to be rude and hyper, (much like Bob). He kept insisting that Bob had "pressured speech," (a common ADD symptom: talking fast in a hyper manner). However, he did not test, make a diagnosis, or prescribe anything. After two sessions, we were quite annoyed and moved on.

We tried another mental health professional about a half hour away. After a couple of visits, he decided that Bob should be tested for ADD, to which we readily agreed. By then I had heard more about ADD being an inherited disorder. He sent Bob to a specialized testing center. After many written and oral tests, they concluded Bob did not have ADD. It seemed they based this opinion mostly on the fact that he was not distracted by traffic noises coming from the open windows during the written tests. I guess they never heard of "hyper-focusing"!

Due to those results, the doctor concluded that Bob must be bipolar instead, in spite of having none of the symptoms. (He was never depressed nor had the highs and lows associated with being bipolar.) This psychiatrist ignored the fact that our son had been diagnosed with ADD, and that I felt strongly there was an inherited connection. He staunchly insisted Bob take medication for this new bipolar diagnosis.

Not only did those pills not work, they made him dizzy and nauseous. The doctor also insisted he show up twice monthly and meet with a psychologist in his office for behavioral training sessions. That proved to be a complete waste of time. Then Bob became so ill from the drugs that he had to stop taking them in order to function. He was so disgusted by this misdiagnosis that he said, “No more doctors.” I really didn’t blame him, but still we needed answers.

For weeks, Bob refused to discuss this matter. Meanwhile, he was still exhibiting many ADD symptoms and continuing his socially embarrassing behavior. I was getting testy because we had not resolved any of our long-standing issues. Bob finally agreed that if I acquired new or different information, he “might” continue pursuing the matter. His challenge encouraged me to continue my research—difficult, as I was not yet using a computer. But, I was very motivated.

Enter our son Scott! He came for a visit

and insisted that his dad try his ADD drug—Ritalin. Since I was absolutely sure Bob had ADD, in spite of the test results being negative, we thought why not try it. If Ritalin is not effective or causes any negative reaction, it's a short lived situation. The stimulant would be out of his system in a matter of hours. Well, guess what? The Ritalin worked like magic. Bob felt fine. He was calm, controlled, focused, and nice! This was a "bingo" moment for the three of us.

Next, we saw the psychiatrist and told him of this experiment. Self-medicating, even though it worked, made him furious. But he did write a prescription for Ritalin. While not pleased with this inept doctor, we were relieved to have Bob on a drug that made such a positive difference. We, his family, were very excited with this finding and accepted the fact that he had ADD. However, while it answered a lot of questions regarding his past behavior, I was not sure that Bob himself was totally convinced of this diagnosis.

Meanwhile, as I diligently continued researching, I picked up some interesting literature about a group called CHADD, a national support group for children and adults with ADD. Since the local chapter was relatively close by, we decided to go to a meeting.

We found the monthly CHADD sessions extremely helpful, and felt that by listening to others, we were not alone. Many adults talked about their children's problems. These sessions convinced several of those parents that they, too, had ADD. Unfortunately, the group disbanded about three months later. Luckily, I had collected business cards from the psychologists who had come to speak. I was able to tap into their knowledge even a year later. The group facilitator was also an excellent source for information. I wish I had known of this support group sooner.

Some weeks after closing, the former CHADD leader gave me the name of an excellent psychiatrist who specialized in Adult ADD, located about forty-five minutes away. Dr. O turned out to be the one who finally and definitively diagnosed Bob! He was a maverick in this field, and we are thankful to this day that we found him when we did. (Sadly, he died a couple of years later, at age forty-five. We still miss him.)

On our first visit in late 2002, this enlightened mental health professional questioned Bob and me closely, establishing that Bob would definitely benefit from his help. Bob had just turned sixty-five, and I was almost sixty-one. At last, we had an official diagnosis and explanation of what caused Bob's bizarre behavior. Finally, after years of research, we found the right doctor to treat his Adult ADD!

Dr. O also shared sad stories of other ADD patients with us. One tale was of a high-ranking military man, who surprisingly became a helpless, homeless street person when he left the structure of army life. Living an ADD life without a caring mentor is extremely challenging.

Two days each week, Dr. O served as a volunteer in the prisons. He said that a large percentage of inmates were afflicted also, which was likely an underlying cause of their incarceration. It quickly became more apparent to us that without a good support system or dedicated family help it can be extremely difficult for ADD people to navigate through modern life. Evidently, street drugs (and even caffeine) are the stimulants that many ADD prisoners used, not knowing they were self-medicating—and not in a good way. Drug and related problems, like stealing to support their expensive habits, were common to this population.

Dr. O had an entirely different approach to treatment. He said if someone has ADD he has it twenty-four hours a day, not just eight or sixteen. This person needs to medicate continuously in order to prevent the lows, (when the drug is wearing off) known as "crashing".

When Ritalin is almost out of the system, the body goes into a free falling mode, like dropping off a building. To lessen this crash, another dose, full or partial, is needed. The size of the dose depends on the time of day or a patient's particular requirements, thus preventing agitation, anger, grumpiness, and stress. These negative traits affect not only the patient, but the people around them, too. The doctor also prescribed a higher and more appropriate dosage of Ritalin for Bob than he had been taking.

According to Dr. O, those with ADD cannot possibly "try harder" to harness their condition. It's similar to expecting someone who wears eyeglasses to try harder to see, or just to squint more. It doesn't work. ADD is truly a brain malfunction with the patient not even aware of being out of control. Putting Bob on a higher level of medication worked well. Dr. O said if a patient doesn't reach the therapeutic dose, which varies with everyone, he or she is not being properly treated. That made perfect sense to us.

We had to search to find a pharmacy that would agree to fill Bob's prescription for the higher than the standard quantity prescribed by most doctors. Only because it caused sleeping problems for Bob did he stop taking his bedtime pills shortly after. The new daytime dose worked just fine though, and our life improved tremendously.

I am not saying our life was perfect, but it was so much better. I could easily tell if Bob forgot to take a pill or when it was wearing off: the grouchy, edgy symptoms would quickly return. Amazingly, he never felt any different, whether he took his pills or not, nor was he aware of how much more civil he was on the medication. However, Bob did notice that when he took his pills I seemed much happier! That was absolutely true.

We were fortunate to be in Dr. O's care for two years. But after this progressive doctor's passing, we needed to find other help quickly. There was such a limited pool of decent local psychiatrists that we took a chance on one that was new to the area.

Our first visit was incredibly unsatisfactory, but still we needed someone willing to prescribe Ritalin. When I asked what experience and knowledge this physician had regarding Adult ADD, her response was to ask me to leave the room! That had never happened to us before and was an indication to me that she knew nothing about this disorder. In fact, she claimed that she could "look-up" whatever she needed to know!

This doctor demonstrated the exact behavior of the type of mental practitioner to avoid. Let me clearly state that if a mental health facilitator does not allow a spouse or significant other to remain in the room, at least initially, just move on. Those who are mentally impaired are seldom capable of explaining or judging their condition, especially when they are getting acquainted with a new doctor. It can be an overwhelming and stressful experience. They need someone who can organize information for that crucial first visit, making sure that important facts are not omitted—or distorted.

After a couple of useless visits with this doctor—that I was not allowed to attend—we finally requested help from our primary physician. He was willing to write the prescriptions since we offered him Bob's records, diagnosis, and drug schedule.

I can't stress how important it is to deal with professionals who are experienced with and accept the existence of Adult ADD. It is imperative they understand that it presents quite differently from ADD in children.

If you or someone you know is hesitant about taking ADD medications for fear of changing who you really are, the following might allay that concern. I posed that key question to a neurologist, who later in this decade managed Bob's condition. I wanted to know which personality represented the "real Bob". Was he the gentle, focused, nice man on drugs, or the grouchy, impatient, ill-tempered guy when not?

The doctor's answer was clear and simple: the "real Bob" is the one on medication. Ritalin, which is a stimulant, supplements brain function and allows the patient to perform more normally, almost as if he did not have a problem. Thus, technically, he is likely representing his true self. I found this somehow comforting.

Part 2

As 2003 began, Bob had a temporary job

that paid quite well, but only for about two months. Without a pension, he really needed to continue working indefinitely. True retirement was not something he could hope to enjoy after our financially disastrous years in the 90s.

Unfortunately, due to increasingly sophisticated technology, real estate companies no longer needed my services, and my small publishing business had become obsolete.

I then focused on improving Bob's mental issues. I figured that while medication helped with ADD, it would be wise to have a good psychologist to talk with from time to time to keep Bob on track. One of the child psychologists we met at a CHADD meeting recommended a colleague who was quite knowledgeable about Adult ADD.

We both liked Dr. D. He was perfect for us from the beginning. He was able to offer perspective on old issues that we had never resolved. One of the first things he did was to explain to Bob, in detail, what a devastating tragedy the bankruptcy had been for me. This was the first time Bob seemed to comprehend my feelings! Before this therapy session, he never seemed to grasp how much, or why, it affected me so deeply.

We went to see Dr. D over the next few years whenever I felt we needed his assistance. The appointments were for Bob, but in reality, they were more like marriage counseling sessions since we both participated. He was able to clarify things to Bob that I knew but could not get him to understand. As is often the case, people listen to outsiders differently. Bob liked and listened well to Dr. D, which was a blessing for me.

The doctor was very impressed with how cooperative Bob was. He was amazed that he sat quietly while I vented, and then readily agreed with me on the validity of most of those complaints. Bob said that remaining quiet, without interrupting, was the least he could do; that he owed me that much for being the cause of my difficult life. The doctor often said he knew he was dealing with two people who loved each other, in spite of tough ongoing issues.

In the spring of 2003, while helping Bob with a job search, I noticed a few advertisements for insurance agents. Since one well-known insurance company was willing to sponsor him, Bob decided to get his license to sell life and health insurance. At last, maybe a permanent new career was possible. He studied diligently for the state test, passed, and became a trainee. But that did not work out. Attempts to sell life insurance through “so called” arranged appointments set up by the company were discouraging. Most people were not interested, and many were not even home when he arrived. He quit.

Luckily, I noticed that a local life and

health insurance broker Bob had briefly worked for (but not as an agent) was starting a new program. It involved insurance agents selling nationally from the office by computer, phone, and fax. This was a perfect fit for Bob, and being close to home was a nice perk. He was hired in June 2003. After becoming comfortable selling life and health insurance, all went well, employment-wise, for several years. He earned a worthwhile income (commission only) and adjusted his hours to fit in his morning tennis games.

In fact, Bob was suddenly playing better tennis, too, which he attributed to Ritalin. That medication, in addition to controlling many of his ADD issues, now provided him better hand and eye coordination. What a nice bonus! Life was starting to improve again. But, we never seemed to remain lucky for long.

It was on a late September morning in 2003 when I woke up with a terrible stomach ache, so painful that I realized this was something serious. I called Bob and told him I needed to go to the hospital immediately. Just saying those words felt strange, but my instincts told me I was in big trouble. I had had a routine colonoscopy just a couple of months before, but I had not felt well since. My colonoscopy results had been fine (so the doctor said), but since I was not feeling well in the following weeks, I visited both my primary care physician and gynecologist. Neither could pinpoint any problem. Since I told them my recent colonoscopy results were fine it was puzzling to them.

At the hospital, it was determined that my colon had ruptured, and I was quickly being poisoned by peritonitis. A surgeon performed surgery on me early that evening. I woke up in the ICU with multiple tubes attached to my body, as well as the dreaded colostomy bag. I was immersed in a nightmare, and was not even sure I was going to live.

Drifting in and out of consciousness, I told Bob, to "Get me out of this hospital immediately!" Of course, that was ridiculous, but I was so worried about the cost until Bob reminded me that we had rather decent health insurance.

During many painful days in the hospital, I began to wonder how Bob was going to handle taking care of me at home. I had always feared that if I ever became seriously ill I would be up the proverbial creek without a paddle. He never had much patience for me being "under the weather". He had never prepared food beyond a sandwich, nor had he done many household tasks either.

Well, I need not have worried at all! I came home and was lovingly pampered by Bob. Visiting nurses tended to me several days a week. On days the nurses were not there, Bob, who learned from them exactly what to do, seamlessly took over. They were not such pleasant tasks either. He rarely left my side for the first weeks. I said many silent prayers of gratitude that Ritalin was now part of our life!

Bob could not possibly have handled any part of this unpleasant situation before starting on meds, which was only months earlier. Fortunately, friends and neighbors responded with much food and love. I am still grateful for the outpouring of help offered to us. What a great community we were living in.

As soon as I came home from the hospital, I called the gastroenterologist's office, told them of my predicament, and requested a copy of the report of my colonoscopy. It just made no sense to me that I was told I was fine following the procedure and then ended up with ruptured colon only weeks later.

When the report arrived I could not believe the diagnosis. The report stated "chronic moderate diverticulosis." What happened to "fine"? I knew that diagnosis was completely ridiculous since I had had no type of related problems or infections … ever!

While healing, I was enlightened during discussions with savvy medical people and attorneys that my colon had been nicked during the colonoscopy, which resulted in the injured area finally wearing away. The doctor had "conveniently forgotten" to tell me about "the nick."

Mistakes happen, but changing my records and covering up facts are a crime! Many horror stories were told to me by this doctor's other victims over the next few years, those lucky enough to have survived his incompetence.

Several weeks later, I had reconstructive surgery to eliminate the colostomy bag. My son said this was probably the only time I would ever eagerly look forward to major surgery. He was so right about that. I could not wait to get rid of "the bag." However, this was truly a more painful experience than the previous emergency surgery.

Our devoted daughter insisted on coming from Massachusetts the day after my release from the hospital. Ava felt we were overwhelmed, and although Bob was doing fine, her visit was a blessing. She cooked, cleaned, and nurtured us both. I am convinced I survived not only because I had been in excellent health to begin with, but had many caring people in my life as well.

I left the hospital this second time in much pain and with a massive amount of stitches. Shockingly, I also had an open hole in my stomach where the colostomy bag had been, big enough to easily hold a golf ball! This hole was deliberately left open to heal slowly from the bottom up to prevent infection. Again, on days without my wonderful visiting nurses, there was "Nurse Bob" carefully cleaning and dressing this layman's "nightmare of a wound". The patience and care he showed me during this trying time was awesome. I recall one day I had a stomach ache that was so dire

I thought I was dying after all. Bob brought me ginger tea and lay quietly on the bed holding my hand for hours until the pain finally subsided. Once again, I was so grateful for Ritalin.

As I got stronger some weeks later, Bob would go into the office part of most days. He needed to get back to work even though it would be months before I was fully healed. I required a third surgery the following year, this time for a large hernia caused by the previous two operations. This was not quite as tough a procedure, but I knew now that I could expect support from Bob. Normally we both shy away from taking medications as much as possible, but with Bob's use of Ritalin, we began to enjoy some peace—finally—and a semblance of normalcy in our life. I then thought ... too bad we did not know of this drug forty-plus years earlier. How much easier our existence would have been. (This was, of course, before our miraculous discovery in 2011.)

In spite of having health insurance, those three surgeries still cost us multi-thousands in deductibles and co-insurances. That was financially very difficult for us. Although we and everyone we knew were convinced I had a valid lawsuit, I was never able to sue to recoup any of my loss. Several lawyers explained to me that I technically had a case, but the new Florida law, which had a cap on pain and suffering reimbursement, prevented them (financially) from taking cases like mine. The litigation costs could easily overtake the amount that the cap allowed.

On recommendation from all those lawyers to do so, I filed a formal complaint complete with 400 pages of medical records with the State Board of Health against the offending doctor. Strangely, eight months later I received a form letter saying they refused to accept my complaint. It was as if it never happened!

I realized right then that it was imperative that I put the physical and mental pain of this nightmare behind me in order to move on. All that remains today are some faded scars, occasional scar tissue pain, and of course, wonderful memories of Bob's fantastic nurturing and care.

At that stage of our life, and after this near death experience, we felt we were bonded forever no matter what. However, when Bob's symptoms reappeared later in this decade, I did give pause to that thought.

There were to be two more procedures for me and two surgeries for Bob before the end of 2010. During those particularly demanding times, Bob's ADD was seemingly not under control any more. I was puzzled by this, as we had not changed his treatment. However, we had little time or energy to address that then.

Part 3

Shortly after moving to Florida in 1998, Bob began having painful stomach issues. Periodically, he seemed to have such awful waves of severe abdominal pain that he would lie on the floor moaning for hours until they passed. A couple of times I took him to the hospital, often against his wishes. (Must be a macho thing.) But they found nothing specific.

After my surgeries in 2003, we found a new gastroenterologist, one we could trust. On a routine visit to this doctor a couple of years later, I happened to mention that ever since I knew Bob, his stomach never seemed to function normally. Bob never discussed this lifelong issue with any physician. He always insisted he was fine and this was normal for him. This was yet another case of unawareness and denial as to what “normal” really is. The doctor’s interest was piqued however, and he immediately ordered tests for Crohn’s disease.

The colonoscopy and lab tests revealed Crohn’s disease, which was the cause of his many agonizing intestinal clogs. Crohn’s is serious autoimmune disease involving the small intestine, and is both chronic and incurable. Evidently, over the years his body was never able to absorb many of the nutrients he ingested. Finally, at age 69, he had an explanation as to why he could not easily gain or maintain weight throughout his life, no matter how much food he consumed.

If Bob had mentioned this problem to a doctor along the way, he would have received an earlier diagnosis, treatment, a proper diet, and avoided some of those excruciating and very dangerous intestinal blockages. We now faced dealing with special foods as well as medications for both diabetes and Crohn's disease. Because the diets somewhat conflict, cooking became much more challenging.

Ironically, the same gastroenterologist who nearly killed me during my colonoscopy had performed that same procedure on Bob a few years earlier, too. We requested a copy of those records after this latest discovery. They clearly showed Crohn's disease was obvious then, but that incompetent doctor never mentioned a single word about it.

Over the years, Bob disagreed with me that he had any of his existing ailments—ADD, diabetes, and Crohn's disease—and he fought me on each one ... all the way to the official diagnosis. How ADD is that?

Part 4

Bob, who loved to play tennis constantly, was quickly wearing out his right hip. He was so obsessed (as in hyper-focused), that he was on the courts about four hours daily. You would think he was practicing for Wimbledon, but no, he was just trying to improve his game with a bunch of retirees. Any suggestion on my part that perhaps he was overdoing it for a person in his 60s was met with the terse retort, "You're always picking on me. You just don't like me playing tennis!"

Until he started selling health insurance in 2003, tennis remained his daily four hour super-focused activity. His hip caused him much pain and prevented him from doing many activities. But, he said that when he was on the tennis court nothing ever hurt. Right, like I believed that!

I was always on the lookout for new and helpful ADD information. Luckily, I found an easy to read educational book, one which clearly demonstrated—using everyday situations as examples—how ADD people unknowingly offend others. This narrative offered great examples for those afflicted as they tend not to understand the negative results or feelings their poor conduct creates. This book would be useful in any ADD household, as it is filled with practical advice for home, work and social situations. I gave this book to Bob and suggested he keep an open mind while reading it. I suspected there was some wishful thinking on his part and that privately he never believed he had ADD. He seemed to be taking his medication only to humor me.

After reading *What Does Everybody Else Know That I Don't*, by Michele Novotni, Ph.D,

Bob was totally convinced he did indeed have a problem. He identified so closely with the social skill examples in the book that he had to concede to his ADD diagnosis after all. He agreed that reading this particular paperback afforded him his defining moment of recognition and acceptance. I recommend this book, especially to those in doubt or denial.

After years of hip discomfort, there was Bob finally having surgery in the spring of 2008. The insurance business was quite lucrative, right up to the day he was admitted to the hospital. Because he worked on commission, he hated to take the time off. The surgery went well, but he had a slow recuperation even with excellent therapy. It is possible that the diabetes slowed his healing process. It was well over a year before the pain subsided enough for him to play tennis or take walks again. But he was able to go back to work in a month. However, business seemed to have suddenly slowed tremendously.

Meanwhile, only weeks after Bob's surgery, another medical problem was brewing, this time for me. I experienced much stress during my life (not unlike many others), and at some point that can cause serious havoc to your body, mind, and spirit.

In the late 90s I began to have panic attacks and palpitations. Initially I was told it was a benign condition. But as time went on the arrhythmias progressed, and in April

2008 it was necessary that I wear a heart monitor for a few weeks. This was inconvenient, but, lucky me, I ended up wearing it for less than twenty-four hours. I was rushed to the hospital that first night with an uncontrolled heart rate of 175 and diagnosed with atrial fibrillation (A-Fib). Bob, barely six weeks post hip-replacement surgery, complete with his cane and pain pills, stayed overnight with me that first scary night.

I remained in the hospital for five days to be monitored while taking a blood thinner and heart medication. How timely it was that Bob and I had made a recent pledge not to be hospitalized at the same time! By the time I was discharged, he was still recuperating, thoroughly exhausted, and had much trouble hobbling around. Leaving the hospital, I helped him into the passenger seat of the car. Feeling quite well again, I carried my own gear and jumped into the driver's seat. As we drove off we giggled, saying anyone watching this scene would have thought Bob had been the patient and I was his driver.

I disliked taking a blood thinner, and the heart pills did not work well. A few months later I decided to have a heart catheter ablation, which offers hope for an A-Fib cure. This tricky, (often four-hour) procedure uses radio waves to burn away the small offending areas of the heart. It is performed in a special lab by a heart specialist trained to do this incredible procedure. I was scheduled to go home the day after. Once again, I was going to need to rely on Bob for care.

I did fine on the day of surgery, but the next morning my palpitations returned with a vengeance, my temperature spiked, and at one point my normally low blood pressure dropped to a dangerous, life-threatening level. Bob ended up spending that night in the hospital on a chair next to my bed and tended to my needs, giving immediate attention as required. You may not think this a big deal for a spouse, but for Bob it was. This, of course, brought more praise from me yet again, grateful for Ritalin.

Meanwhile, my runaway pulse would not respond to any medication. The doctor wanted to try a rather dangerous drug in my IV drip, which, because of the risk, would require him to stay with me until it was finished. I refused; it just seemed too unsafe.

When a friend called a short time later I asked that she contact others in our circle. Together they held a conference call and prayed for me that evening. It worked! Early the following morning my temperature and blood pressure had returned to normal, and, best of all, my heart rate was just fine. Happily, I went home with heartfelt gratitude to some very special women.

Complete healing from a heart ablation takes about six months. However, my health started to deteriorate quickly again after only a few weeks. I was not doing well with the blood thinner or the heart medication either, both of which are still needed while healing. I also had developed a severe shoulder problem due to awkward positioning of my arm during the ablation. That painful issue alone took weeks of treatment to fix.

At this time, Bob began exhibiting many of the ADD symptoms that had caused me much stress over the years, putting my heart health in even more danger. Bob was no longer such a big help now! He reverted to his old agitated and unaware state even though he was still faithfully taking his meds. I was getting annoyed because these ADD incidents seemed to be occurring daily. I felt we should seek immediate help. A visit to our psychologist Dr. D was needed to put order back into our lives.

The day of that appointment, I left to run errands and Bob went to work. As I was leaving I mentioned the specific Kangaroo gas station we would meet at three hours later. We would leave one car there so we could travel the rest of the forty-minute drive together. Almost ten minutes past our meeting time, there was no sign of Bob. He is seldom late for anything, so this was odd. I called, and he said he was at another station about two miles further away from our destination. (He had not called me though to see where I was.) He swore he was at the agreed upon location, but it was a grungy no-name facility that I would never have chosen. How hard is it to remember the unusual name Kangaroo? He also repeated that name to me three hours earlier.

We were now obviously going to be late for this much-needed appointment. We argued all the way to the psychologist's office and called to alert him of our delay. We were a half hour late, paid for the full hour, and confused Dr. D about "who did what wrong." What a waste of a visit. But the good doctor was able to calm us both before we left. Bob agreed later that I would never have chosen such a dilapidated place to leave a car.

During this abbreviated session, Dr. D was quite concerned about my heart health and suggested that Bob be more mindful of this serious issue and the extreme stress he was continuously causing me. Bob seemed to understand.

But a week later, and after a few more of his uncontrolled ADD episodes, I was again rushed to our local hospital with wild palpitations. They could not be controlled, so the next day it was necessary to take me by ambulance to the hospital about twenty-five minutes away where the special ablation laboratory was located. My heart specialist made all the arrangements for the second ablation and would be there for my arrival. Bob was to follow in his car and meet me there.

Ambulances arrive at their destinations

quickly. A half hour later I was in my hospital room, getting prepped, waiting for the doctor to come in to discuss the plan and time for this necessary second ablation. Where was Bob? Another hour plus passed, and still no Bob. I worried that he had been in an accident. I did not have my cell phone with me and could not remember his number without my auto dial. Where on earth was he? My heart was racing from my condition. This was making it much worse.

It turned out that Bob was sitting in the lobby of the hospital, patiently waiting for the ambulance to arrive while I was livid yet very nervous in my room regarding his whereabouts. Finally, after waiting more than an hour, he decided to find out where I might be! He then sat by my bed trying to explain why he was waiting so long downstairs, but I had no interest in listening to his lame explanation.

Meanwhile the doctor came in and sat in the only other available chair, which was behind Bob. So the doctor would not have to crane his neck just to talk to me I had to ask Bob to move. He was acting so spacey. During this hospital stay I told him that we were going to have to consider moving back north near our kids so I would have responsible family nearby in case of an illness or emergency, such as this. I felt like we were going backwards in time.

Thankfully, the procedure went fine this

time and I went home the next day. After a few minor issues during the healing process I was cured, forever I hope, and grateful to my excellent doctor. I was able to eliminate all medications and feel fortunate today to be healthy again. But I knew as soon as I was feeling better it would be necessary, yet again, to revisit whatever problems were going on with Bob.

Part 5

While still healing from my second ablation, Bob began experiencing intestinal clogs and stomach pains again. We knew it was time to consider the inevitable—Crohn's disease surgery. This is a major procedure, which involves removing the affected areas of the small intestine. It is not a cure, since there isn't one, but a "clean up" of the diseased areas. Bob had this surgery on Dec 23, 2009.

At the end of the year, there were always financial matters with December 31st deadlines that Bob needed to tend to. I suggested he take care of all such business before his December 23rd surgery. One never knows what delays might happen when going into a hospital setting. He saw that as unnecessary because he was to be in the hospital only five to seven days.

In his typical ADD style, he insisted he would be home in five days and worry about everything then ... as in "later". Later is a word used by Bob (and others with ADD), one that often gets him into a great deal of trouble. It really means “not now, and don’t bother me about it”. Procrastination!

My first thought was: Who would feel well enough to do any financial dealings the day after coming home from the hospital following major surgery? But it was useless to mention this to Bob.

It so happened he had a tough time recuperating, and his stomach refused to “wake-up”; not so uncommon after this type of operation. He was unable go home until the fourth of January! The projected five to seven day hospital stay ended up being almost two weeks. But Bob seldom has that Plan B.

Three days before his December 31st deadline, he called me in the evening after a long day with him in the hospital. He insisted I bring him my laptop computer in the morning so he could get online to address his fiscal issues. This would not be simple do to since my computer weighed about 20 pounds and I had no case for it. Parking was almost two blocks from the hospital entrance, and he was on the sixth floor. Add to that fact that he was too sick to sit up for more than ten minutes at a time, and his stomach had a very long column of staples holding him together. No way could he have this heavy equipment on his lap. But he insisted and said he had arranged with the hospital to access their Wi-Fi system. He also called our computer savvy son-in-law late in the evening and tersely interrogated him on how to navigate the technical details.

In reality, Bob was having one of those ADD "meltdowns" he was famous for, and taking his frustration out on us, his family. No doubt his Ritalin dose had long since worn off. I told him that I could not possibly lug in the heavy computer and that he would have to manage the accounts in question over the phone. He hung up on me.

He historically has an impatience problem with situations such as being left "on hold" on the phone for an indeterminate period of time. But it was his poor planning and procrastination before going to the hospital that caused this particular emergency in the first place! Last minute crises like this were always happening to him.

The next morning, our daughter, upset by this too, called and suggested I not drag my heavy computer to the hospital. I told her not to worry; I had no intention of doing so, and off I went to the hospital to tell Bob that if he groused at me like that again I would not return until he was to be discharged.

Meanwhile, having taken his morning Ritalin pill before I arrived, Bob apologized and was a perfect gentleman. He was resigned to spending an hour or so on the phone waiting to get his investment details resolved. His call resulted in finding out he had until April 1st to take care of those issues after all!

He should have known. This mess was a perfect example of inattention, poor planning, procrastination, poor decisions, denial, and a grouchy alienating personality, all rolled into one. This is not unusual for someone with ADD. But still, it is always maddening to me anyhow that these people don't seem to understand how selfish and frustrating their ridiculous actions are to others.

Part 6

Bob spent the month of January 2010 recovering at home. Then it was time to return to the office, where business was not good and had not been for more than a year. I was quite concerned and suggested several times during the year that it was undeniably time to be making a job change. But, there he was, routinely continuing to go to the office daily. Maybe it was the comfort of the familiar. Bob generally "got stuck" and remained in hopeless situations even though they no longer worked for him. He was again in denial, just as he was when his Connecticut business was fading away. I know he loved his job, but his income had dwindled to practically nothing.

Then the clincher came. The new health care law killed any hope of revival for health insurance sales. Government rules and the new law had also destroyed the health insurance commission rate structure causing many agents to lose their livelihood.

Bob finally agreed with me that there was no point in going to the office anymore. He definitely needed another job though, but was procrastinating, and was again in stubborn denial about how serious our financial situation was. He said he would look for something but wondered where someone as old as he could hope to find work. I recognized that his age was a problem but insisted he forge ahead and look anyhow. We were not secure retirees and never would be.

I was starting to feel the same terror I experienced in 1997 when Bob allowed the unthinkable to happen to us. Sometimes my fears would take my breath away. I felt trapped, and counting on Bob to step up to the plate was not realistic. We sort of muddled through until summer when we went north to spend time with our family for our 50th wedding anniversary.

I felt minimal joy for this incredible milestone, as my fears were all I could focus on. The situation had an impact on my everyday life as well. I was becoming depressed and started backing away from many of my activities. I was rightfully consumed by severe stress. My lifestyle, home, and financial stability were at risk and there was no safety net. We were also older and poorer than in 1997. Not a good situation at all!

A week before we went north I was

extremely annoyed by Bob's carelessness. He suddenly realized that he had been taking a double dose of glucosamine, and for several months, too. He is such a creature of habit and routine, and he usually does not bother to think about what he is doing.

In addition to taking his usual morning dose, he somehow was mistakenly taking a second dose in the evening. I quickly realized that this was the cause of the breast pain and swelling he had experienced three months earlier, which necessitated the need for a mammogram. Even though those test results were benign, it was a nerve-wracking experience—one evidently caused by his carelessness.

It was mentioned at the mammography center that certain medications can bring on unusual symptoms, especially in men. But who would have thought Bob was taking a double dose of anything? I had him stop cold turkey. (He just wanted to cut back.) Then we looked up the side effects. In addition to breast changes, there was the possibly of injury to the pancreas, which can make diabetic conditions worse. Sure enough, that is what happened, and that damage is often permanent. So his ADD—his attention deficit—was causing him physical injury.

As soon as we returned home from New England, I pleaded with Bob to recognize and address our serious financial circumstances. You can't solve a problem if you deny it exists!

I sat for an entire day explaining this to him. He said I was exaggerating the issue.

I wasn't getting through to him until I thought to insist he check out the figures in our banking records. He said I should have simply told him to do that in the first place, since he then immediately saw our predicament in black and white. Clearly he was unaware of the obvious, and that made no sense to me, as he was the one who organized and kept up with our financial records. Finally, he agreed that we did have a big problem.

However, a few days later he suddenly did a reversal, saying that I was "way over blowing the situation," and again stated that we were financially fine. Huh? I felt sure we were doomed now! I realized he did not comprehend any of this, even though all was still in black and white in our ledgers. What was going on here? How could he not understand? Yet again, he had me feeling confused, angry, and frankly terrified.

I immediately called Dr. D. I desperately hoped someone Bob trusted could explain the facts to him. During that appointment, Dr. D told me he thought possibly something else was going on in addition to ADD, and he felt that anything that needed to be done fiscally from now on should be my responsibility. Since Bob did not seem to grasp this situation, there was nothing further he could do to help us. After all these years, we were now beyond Dr. D's help.

Neither of us spoke on the ride home. I was thinking I would now be dealing with dementia or worse. This all tied in now with Ritalin's failure over the past couple of years. In fact, I had slightly increased his dosage and changed his schedule a few months before, thinking that might help, but it did not. This extreme behavior seems to have started gradually, perhaps between my first and second ablation.

I was so frightened! I already knew firsthand the importance of money. Financial control of one's life? That seemed like an elusive luxury to me!

In the process of formulating my plan to get to the bottom of Bob's newest brain issue, I remembered that the nurse at the hospital told Bob that all his blood work was fine, but to get his B-12 level tested after he was discharged, as many seniors are lacking in this vitamin. We had it checked and it was very low, just barely in the normal range. But his doctor said, since it was in the normal range, it would not be considered deficient.

I got to thinking about that. I had heard low/normal B-12 is "not so fine" and can cause dementia-like symptoms and eventually lead to dementia itself. So Bob was tested again after taking a very high dose of B-12 vitamins, sublingually, (under the tongue) which was suggested as the best way to absorb it, but it was still too low. We since have learned that, with Crohn's disease, as it is with food, afflicted people don't absorb vitamin supplements very well either.

I thought perhaps a psychiatrist could help, thinking a change in the Ritalin dosing might work, as well as getting advice on the vitamin B-12 problem. I was desperate. We could not get a timely appointment to see the rather good mental health provider we had seen only a couple of times about a year before. However, there was another member of that practice available to us.

It was unfortunate that we agreed to meet with this very hyper psychiatrist. He spent most of the six minutes we endured being in his office accusing us of being there "just for drugs." He kept repeating that and in such an agitated manner, too. (Gosh, wonder if he has ADD!) He said that Bob was just fine, did not have ADD, and that he did not believe in giving anyone "that dangerous drug," Ritalin. When he restated all these words for the third time, Bob and I got up and walked out. No help there for sure. This is one more example that not all psychiatrists are sufficiently knowledgeable regarding Adult ADD.

Our next stop was to a naturalist physician who only wanted to perform a multitude of expensive but unrelated tests. No thanks; we left.

Then, by chance, a friend gave me the name of her neurologist, Dr. J, a perfect choice for us, as he was quick and efficient.

He immediately ordered a brain wave, an MRI, and blood work. These tests showed no indication of dementia. What a relief! But Bob's B-12 level was clearly too low and possibly the cause of the worsening ADD and dementia symptoms. Bob began B-12 shots and also a new (to him) ADD drug. This doctor said he probably needed a "holiday" from Ritalin. We switched to Adderall. It is perhaps a smoother drug, with less "crashing" as the pill wears off.

The B-12 shots, twice monthly, were slowly helping. Injections are a big improvement over the capsules because they bypass the small intestine and are better absorbed by a Crohn's disease patient. Still, much effort would be needed to put our exceedingly frazzled, insecure life back in order.

It was in the spring of 2010 that I began writing this memoir as a legacy for our grandchildren and quickly realized it would surely be welcomed and appreciated by a much wider (and needy) audience as well. After discarding my fears of exposure, I quickly changed the book's format and forged ahead, writing about our complex life. It has been both cathartic and painful to relive my past in print, but it felt like the exact thing to do—and the right time to do it.

This decade ended with us happy to be physically healthy again. I had also methodically and successfully restored our low credit score back to A-plus by 2008. But, along with a variety of unresolved ADD situations, there were still severe financial issues looming. Bob needed a job, but at seventy-three it is difficult to find one. We were both feeling the effects of age discrimination. I, too, had applied to interesting job opportunities, but without success. Scary! I certainly didn't feel old.

Ready or not, 2011 included a mixed bag of serious concerns, useless opportunities ... and a miracle!

ADD Notes

Medications can lose their effectiveness after taking them over a long period of time. Consider a change or the possibility that something else may be going on as well.

Since unawareness often involves denial, too, it may be necessary for a mentor to pursue serious matters on behalf of the ADD spouse, in spite of protests. Otherwise, health and safety issues may be compromised.

In general, it is wise to take control of your own health issues. As you can see, medical providers are not always correct or sufficiently knowledgeable. Do your own research. Educate yourself, at least enough to evaluate that your diagnosis and treatment are correct.

I recommend reading *Healing ADD* by Daniel G. Amen, M.D. In this book he discusses the six types of ADD.

Chapter 7 – More ADD Moments "You're Always Picking on me"

Hundreds of well-known scientists, inventors, actors, business moguls, sports players, and American presidents have something of great importance in common with Bob. They, too, have (or had) ADD. In fact, there is an amazingly long list online of famous people with ADD.

We tend to think we know a lot about them because of their public presence, but details concerning how they relate to family and close friends may well be hidden. And so it was with Bob. Almost no one knew what our life was really like.

Quite literally, something ADD related happened every day. It was just a fact of our life. In order to keep my sanity, I tried to pick my battles carefully by ignoring the minor, but still frustrating incidents. Some days that worked; other days, it didn't.

I tried my best to make us look like the family I always wished us to be. While I was successful to a point, it was not without a downside. My life was ruled by constant anxiety as I instinctively strived to help Bob appear to be normal, doing many of the necessary things for him that he was unable to cope with. Privately, I endured his odd ADD way of thinking and behaving.

In our early years, I did not realize exactly *why* I was doing this, but it was the only way I could picture us in a positive light. As time went on, this behavior became my habit—difficult, but necessary in order to maintain some semblance of us as being a typical family.

There were many days that I felt as if Bob was my third child—and the most difficult one at that. If I had a dollar for every time he said, "You're always picking on me," I would be a wealthy woman today. I tolerated that annoying phrase until the day he began taking Ritalin in 2002. Then it stopped cold and everything changed.

Suddenly he was calm, rarely exhibited childish behavior, and he no longer felt that I was picking on him. He called Ritalin a wonder drug, although he felt no different when taking it. He liked that it made me different and happier; but he still didn't quite comprehend that *he* was now the different one!

The following are some of the typical characteristics of this neurobiological disorder. Few ADD people have all of them. It seems that each individual has his (or her) own personal combination ....

Procrastination • denial • agitation • quick temper • impatience • selfishness • social isolation • poor social skills • failure to see others' needs • failure to learn from the past • tantrums • moodiness • inflexibility • unpredictability • meanness/nastiness • impulsiveness • inability to concentrate • poor listening skills • pressured speech • excessive talking • persistent interrupting • forgetfulness • trouble shifting attention • hyper-focusing • anger • irritability • disorganization • not completing projects • oversleeping • tardiness • erratic job history • poor handwriting • addictions • sensitivity to noise or touch • risky behavior • risk taking • stubbornness • poor judgment • general unawareness • poor decision making ... and of course, focusing issues.

****

The examples portrayed here will illustrate the different thinking/acting process that ADD people are known for. Some of their "out-of-the-box" ideas have been wonderful for mankind. Scientists, such as Albert Einstein, who could not speak until he was four, or inventor Thomas Edison, whose teachers said he was too stupid to learn anything, are examples of geniuses who are thought to have had ADD. Another, Walt Disney, was fired by a newspaper editor because he had "no good ideas"!

However, that same unique way of thinking can cause much harm as well. The following are excerpts from our family diary. Living with someone with ADD, you're always waiting for the other shoe to drop. You know it will, you just don't know when!

Poor Listening Skills and Selfishness

In May 1960, two months before we married, Bob ventured out to buy our new family car. In retrospect, I should have gone with him. My parting words when he left were, "Please—do not buy a stick shift!" I knew how to drive, but only an automatic transmission, and had no interest in learning to drive anything else.

But, he returned as the proud owner of a new blue Ford—with a manual transmission. He said he saved $100 by not getting the automatic drive and had forgotten that I specifically requested otherwise. (No, I was definitely not happy.)

It suddenly became necessary that I quickly learn how to drive our new car even though I was totally consumed with handling our wedding details.

I now know that unless Bob repeats certain information back to me, it probably doesn't register in his brain.

Hyper-focusing, Impatience, Risky Behavior and Stubbornness

In the late 60s, while driving our family home in heavy holiday nighttime traffic, Bob became so annoyed by slow moving cars, that he began weaving in and out of the traffic lanes. He was driving fast like an erratic, crazed madman. I was terrified. Asking him to slow down incensed him even more, and he just drove faster. His brain was in overdrive and he couldn't be reached.

Thankfully, a state trooper persevered through the dense traffic to stop us. I was so relieved I almost hugged the officer, who was so upset and horrified upon seeing our children in the back; he asked Bob if he was trying to kill his family! He gave him a stern lecture, but amazingly, no ticket. The trooper, by stopping Bob, defused his super hyper behavior; similar to the effect of a slap in the face. An accident was no doubt averted.

Bob's impatience was always in play when he drove, yet he constantly complained about other drivers. It got to the point that, for my own safety and peace of mind, I started doing the driving when we went anywhere together. It's more relaxing for me, and Bob is okay with this. Many ADD people exhibit risky driving habits.

Unawareness

A few years ago, Bob asked to use my desk for a while. He had a project sprawled out on his and he needed a clear space. That was fine with me ... or so I thought at the time.

The next day I went to look for my date planner-calendar, but it was nowhere to be found. It never leaves my desk and is so important to my life—filled with membership club lists, household papers, appointment calendar, etc.—that I took to calling it my "bible". I also save these multi-functional planners and refer back to them as needed over the next few years.

Bob said he "sort of remembered" something falling into the wastebasket (which was beside the desk), but paid no attention to it. Then we both immediately realized the trash had been emptied, the rubbish was already picked up, and the calendar was on its way to the landfill! Bob called the county for the destined location and wanted to drive the hour away to search through the piles of trash, but learned that was neither practical nor allowed.

My 2004 calendar was lost forever. That was in early October and I labored to resurrect my schedule for the rest of the year. All sorts of my valuable records were now in landfill heaven! I struggled and fumed for weeks. Yes, Bob felt quite badly, but his lack of awareness was so destructive.

Procrastination, Poor Judgment, Risky Behavior and Selfishness

In early 2011 we got a letter that appeared to be junk mail, but since it was from our life insurance company I opened it, even though it was addressed to Bob. Good thing I did! It was a notice stating that the payment for his insurance policy was late, already well into the grace period, and would expire in ten days if payment was not received by then. We had never discussed dropping it, nor would I have agreed to that. We had been paying for term life insurance for 50 years. At Bob's age I was not about to let that lapse.

We have a firm household rule—to pay our bills promptly—so this surprised me. Bob casually said that he was going to pay it next week: "No big deal!" It drives me crazy when he leaves things to the last minute, never projecting the risks involved. (Like his five-day hospital stay that ended up lasting two weeks.) What if he died and I didn't know he had not paid it? Or what if he became ill, requiring an emergency hospital visit? Or, what if his check was simply delayed in the mail and the deadline was missed?

It certainly was a big deal to me! Next thing Bob knew, he was standing in the post office, mailing the check, and requesting proof of delivery and tracking information. The potential of this devastating mess upset me and ruined my mood for several days.

Thinking vs. Rote

Bob decided in early 2011 to help out by doing some household tasks and food preparation. We quickly realized that cooking a meal was too much for him, but I did think he could handle preparing frozen food or reheating leftovers. Since we sometimes have a giant salad with tuna fish or cottage cheese for dinner, he watched me make that, and then wrote down "the recipe". He does a grand job of putting a salad together now, but only if he follows his written recipe—opening a bag of salad greens and slicing up a few vegetables.

I was out grocery shopping one day and running a bit late, which is not unusual for me. Bob was in charge of fixing our dinner that evening. This involved putting prepared fish and cleaned sweet potatoes in the oven and steaming the broccoli—a simple and quick meal. He did fine ... except that he baked the fish and steamed the broccoli long before I came home, and the potatoes were never readied to be cooked at all. He told me this when I called to tell him I would be home in ten minutes, and "don't cook the food till I put the groceries away." Too late! Dinner was already done ... except for the forgotten potatoes. Instead of waiting until the appropriate time, Bob hyper-focused on preparing the meal, and made dinner way too soon.

For Bob, his avoidance of thinking is strongly tied to his unawareness. He is comfortable only with rote, and appears uninterested in "thinking things through". Routine certainly has its place, but not 100% of the time—except maybe for Bob. In this case, he got so caught up in the details of the food preparation that he didn't consider the timing or circumstances.

Procrastination and Risk Taking

Bob had been selling health insurance for several years and is a caring and knowledgeable agent. Every two years he, like all agents, is required to take a Continuing Education test to maintain his license.

This is not a problem for him. He studies what he needs to and does well on the test. But he always waits until the last second to take this exam, which is stressful for me. He does not allot time for the possibility of disruptive or emergency circumstances that often happen to him. This is one of many types of risky behavior common to ADD people.

If Bob misses the test deadline, there is a large fine—and he still needs to take the test anyhow. I had been trying to get him to do this a couple of months ahead so that I don't have this anxiety with every license renewal.

Many other time-sensitive obligations come up, some of which I am not aware of until they become "Bob-created emergencies." For example, our community conducts an annual resident survey. I was interested in participating in the spring of 2011—anxious to offer my input. I kept waiting for our Internet access code to arrive by mail, but wasn't thinking about it until someone mentioned to me that the survey deadline was the next day.

I panicked and was about to make a call suggesting our code number was lost in the mail, when Bob said he had it. It came weeks earlier, but he never told me. He put it away, ridiculously assuming that when I was ready I would ask him for it! Huh? However, by Bob doing this, he also violated our strict household edict. For obvious reasons, I am supposed to see all the incoming mail. He broke this trust, and I almost lost my opportunity to fill in the survey.

Noise Sensitivity

We have several pocket doors in our home. They are great space savers but are more awkward to close than standard doors. If you push or pull too hard they can slam. One day I accidently slammed a door and Bob went ballistic. He carried on and became agitated for much longer than the split second the noise lasted. Suddenly, we had a ruined afternoon!

Automobile directional signals are another

problem. Bob hates the noise of the blinkers so much so that now I rarely use them while stopped waiting for a traffic light to change, only switching them on when I deem it really necessary for safety.

I read recently that noise issues are a characteristic of ADD. I can live with this problem now that I know it exists.

Social Issues and Excessive Talking

Bob and I like to play a variety of card and board games and enjoy wonderful evenings of friendly competition with friends and neighbors. This works well for Bob as he is able to easily focus on this activity.

The problem was, in social settings especially, his excessive talking symptom did sometimes surface, and he just couldn't seem to stop. He could get hung up on a subject of no interest to others, or discuss socially inappropriate topics without being remotely aware that he was doing so. This was unsettling to me and no doubt everyone else.

When this happened I helped him understand his bad manners the next day, and he always insisted on making a phone call to apologize. I appreciated the gracious acceptance and understanding he received from friends.

Over the years, some couples have drifted away from us because of his behavior, especially before 2002 when he started taking

Ritalin. (Bob insists that those who persevered and stuck with us have done so only because they like my company.) More recently we told friends that when he is over-talking to please give him a “time out” signal. He will discontinue immediately ... even in mid-word! Often, he is unable to stop without getting that proverbial “kick in the shins”. (Before he was on Ritalin, nothing stopped him.) This approach has really helped. Since I love to socialize, I really appreciate Bob putting forth his best effort on this issue.

******

There are many “moments” large and small in ADD households. Some are minor, such as when Bob has recorded a movie only to find out he recorded the wrong channel just as we settled in to watch it.

People often say to me: “Everyone does these things.” Yes, they do! The difference is, those with ADD do them constantly, rather than occasionally.

Bob is, in fact, quite intelligent and knowledgeable, but sadly he does suffer with this extremely difficult disorder. Although many times I fantasized about leaving for a better life, I always felt that it was my destiny to take care of him. You just don’t leave someone because they are ill, physically or mentally ... at least I don’t.

Chapter 8 - 2011
The Road Less Traveled

The year 2011 started out instantly stressful. Disappointments were coming at us left and right. We could not seem get a handle on life, mostly because nothing was in our control.

Bob, who had switched to Adderall (from Ritalin) in late 2010, had become dull and passive. He went back to Ritalin, which helped some, but this change did not prevent him from exhibiting a myriad of ADD gaffes, including poor decision-making. We were also concerned about his lack of employment. I was nervous all the time with alternating days of optimism and pessimism.

Bob was approached to sell for a large insurance brokerage firm that "promised the moon." He signed on, but the moon never materialized and he resigned a month later. However, without discussing it with me, and at the firm's insistence, he had foolishly signed up for a six-month commitment to use their Internet web conferencing tool. He nixed the option of buying it for one month at a time (at a higher cost), which would have been the better way to try it out, while also evaluating the company.

However, that company would not let him cancel this contract after he left and insisted he pay for the remaining five months even though he no longer had access to the product. We needed to bring in income, but Bob was carelessly increasing our outgo!

I was incensed and decided to fight this ridiculous agreement, one that was automatically adding a significant amount to our charge card expenses every month. This mess involved weeks of telephoning and writing letters to Visa to resolve this complicated financial blunder. This was yet one more example of our famous funky dance.

After that exhausting fiasco, Bob contacted his former insurance agency employer saying he would be happy to work from home if there was any ongoing business. He was sent a few leads, but had little success. The health insurance business was still floundering nationally. Bob pursued other employment and went out on a couple of interviews. Age discrimination was no doubt a factor in his lack of offers.

In June, his former employer called to say that that several promising opportunities appeared to be developing, which should result in greatly increased business, starting in July. In fact, special phone lines had been installed in the office to accommodate the huge volume of expected callers.

By September, however, nothing had come

of this. Although Bob had asked, no answers seemed available as to what was (not) happening. Therefore, for us, it was back to square one.

Meanwhile, Bob's daily, mostly minor ADD infractions seemed constant and relentless. Many mornings before I was up and dressed several ridiculous incidents had already taken place. It created a bad start to my day. Bob recognized (after some "lively discussion") that he does odd, non-thinking, and annoying things, and admitted that he doesn't seem to be able to control these actions. He still continued to underestimate our financial woes as well. For my sanity I was thinking that Bob needed to be elsewhere other than home, such as at a job, at least part of the day.

I spoke with his neurologist, but he had nothing new to offer—no suggestions or different medications. Our immediate future was quite precarious on many levels.

While I still felt young and vibrant, the main core of my soul had been very one-dimensional and wasted over the decades with many ongoing fears, especially for our financial survival. I often surprised myself, possessing such a fierce determination to continue on. I certainly had grown stronger as the years passed, but by 2011 I was feeling so tired and defeated, having "been there, done that" far too many times.

It seemed that we had reached the limit of

what the medical community could do to help with Bob's ADD problem. I was desperate for more options. Never one to completely give up, I wistfully thought an alternative solution might somehow be found. I guess I was hoping for a miracle.

In early July, there was a notice about a dowsers club meeting in our area. Dowsing with a pendulum is simply a means of getting information and help regarding health and many other issues. In countries where water sources are scarce, dowsing with a rod or forked stick is a highly respected profession. It is used to find water and test it for purity.

A friend showed me how to use a pendulum to get answers to simple questions a couple of years before, but still I knew only a smattering about this subject. Being curious, I attended the session. I could not have imagined the impact this gathering would have on me.

Some of the members talked about a gifted teacher and healer, a mountain man who had spoken at the recent dowser's annual convention they attended. Raymon Grace[4] is well known internationally for his success in teaching people how to take control of their life and health through dowsing.

After the meeting, I asked how I could connect with Raymon. Hearing about only a few of his abilities and techniques, I was

---

[4] Raymon Grace, author of *The Future is Yours—Do Something About It.* www.raymongrace.us

anxious to find out what he could do for ADD. After all, Bob's medication was not working well. Although it kept him from being agitated and angry, and the calmness was wonderful, his other symptoms were definitely not under control. He had been unable to live a normal life for far too long.

Attending a dowsing class a couple of weeks later, taught by the club president, I was convinced this was something worthwhile to pursue, and with its relationship to science it was quite intriguing, too. Users feel that dowsing is a consequence of the laws of quantum physics: since everything in the universe is interconnected, dowsing is simply a way of tuning in to the quantum field. This was an educational experience.

At the next monthly meeting, we watched a Raymon Grace video on healing. It was amazing to hear him discuss the symptoms of ADD, although he never called it that. He said many people desperately reaching out for his help are those who live with folks that exhibit "abnormal behavior". (But he never hears from those afflicted!) I completely identified with the abnormal behavior and desperate callers.

I emailed Raymon saying that I suspected many of those calls involved ADD, a condition that he and many of his callers were not seemingly familiar with. He said he hadn't realized this until I pointed it out. His reaction: "Then the world is in big trouble," as he recognized how widespread the problem was. But it didn't matter what the condition was officially called, he felt he could help anyhow.

As I watched that video, Raymon grabbed my full attention by explaining that one of the main reasons people do not "behave well" is because the blood to the brain is not flowing properly, nor are the right and left brain hemispheres balanced. What happened next was to become life changing for Bob and me.

As a random act of kindness, Raymon checked out Bob (from his mountain home in Virginia) by dowsing for answers. He sent me a rather long list of faults he found, (including the important brain balancing/blood flow issue) which were causing Bob's negative behavior; such as his body was vibrating on the wrong frequency and his life blueprint was unbalanced. Bottom line: he said Bob was an energetic wreck! He sure got that right!

Through dowsing, he fixed all that he found, and said that some of these fixes would be permanent. He said the remainder would need tweaking, but that I could do that for Bob myself, by dowsing. Being a trained engineer, it was a big leap for Bob to embrace this concept. But thankfully, he did! So the pendulum I casually enjoyed using for the previous two years was to become a healing tool for Bob as well.

Now for the uplifting news: What Raymon Grace did for Bob appears to have worked. It adjusted his thinking process and behavior. Thank you, Raymon! I can't explain the "why or how," but to quote inventor Thomas Edison: "What's electricity? Well, I don't know, but it's there, so let's use it."

Bob's results were quick and remarkable. He became aware that he was effortlessly changing for the better, and that I was now a very happy person. Revealing a new persona, he seemed to be doing all the right things. He began taking initiative—looking to quick accomplishment instead of procrastination. I asked if he was making a concerted effort to try harder, but Bob insisted he wasn't, and realistically, we both knew that "trying harder" was not something he was able to do.

We agreed that he would remain on Ritalin (although truthfully, not very effective anymore) as we savored the healing benefits from dowsing. It was almost two weeks later that we were out doing some annoying but necessary errands, which Bob normally avoids. However, he offered to help, and had a new and cheerful attitude. That demeanor lasted right through the sudden demise of our car battery just as we were about to drive home. He steadfastly managed that tiresome day better than I did.

I was wondering where the "original Bob" was at this point. He looked like the guy I had known for over fifty years, but he evidently had been replaced by a new and improved version.

The next day he asked how I thought he was doing. "Just great," I said! And then he told me ... he had not taken a Ritalin pill for the last three days. I was stunned by his experiment. He was more grounded than he had been since I had known him. My cup runneth over!

Bob's new demeanor remained just fine for the next three months. I was dowsing a couple of times a day to keep his brain balanced and the blood flowing, which takes only a minute or two daily. (Bob seemed unable to use the pendulum; it simply would not work for him.)

Then, over a two week period in December, he reverted back to his former ADD status. This was so disheartening that I was visibly shaken. What was going on? I was not up to managing any further disappointment. Bob knew this, too, as I was not-so-quietly lamenting for several days. Although he had no explanation, he agreed he was acting poorly again.

Because I attended one of Raymon's inspiring two day workshops in late October, I had benefit of knowing much of what he does—and teaches others to do—but was feeling much too defeated and depressed to function. This was, after so many valiant attempts for a normal life, a huge letdown.

Then an amazing thing happened! Since I had explained to Bob much of what I learned when I returned from the workshop, he abruptly grabbed my book, notes, and charts and decided that he would heal himself! He was already convinced that dowsing does work and that it offered us our best chance for a harmonious life. But since he had been unable to get the pendulum to work I had no idea why he thought he would succeed in this endeavor. But heal himself he did!

He spent the next two days working on this project ... alone. He was so fiercely determined; he somehow managed to get his pendulum working after all. Then, by dowsing, he checked the extensive list of influences that might be causing this problem, just as Raymon had done. He found much in need of correction by dowsing. (Perhaps I had missed something ... I don't know.)

After working diligently on the second day, and checking out his previous day's work, Bob proudly announced that he and the pendulum were in complete agreement: that all was cleared and he was again healed. Indeed he was! The "new Bob" was back as if the setback had never happened. He is now in charge, and on a daily basis maintains this situation by dowsing—keeping his brain balanced and blood flowing freely—to keep the ADD demon away. He also does a periodic check of the complete list to sustain his success.

I hope this unpleasant setback is never repeated, but at least Bob knows exactly how to handle it now. (Good for me, I deserve a break!) Both of us are keeping an open mind as we continue our journey on this road less traveled.

Raymon Grace says he doesn't heal people, but teaches them how to heal themselves. He conducts his workshops throughout the country to educate and share his knowledge. I am fortunate and grateful that he took a personal interest in helping Bob and me. According to Raymon: "If you do nothing, nothing is going to happen; if you do something, something might happen. The future is yours, do something about it."

Desire for success has been the driving force in my life, always. Success, however, was defined in many different ways over the last 50 plus years. Sometimes it meant keeping Bob focused and productive. Other times it involved creating security for our children, growing my business, or getting Bob's medical conditions diagnosed in spite of his resistance.

Then, in mid-2011, my purpose changed. While observing and listening to the youngest generation of Rosenbaums, I realized our teenage grandchildren were (rightfully) concerned about their family heredity. They worried about spawning ADD babies of their own and began talking of possibly never reproducing. Now I had a new reason to be angry! Theirs would be the first generation in our family that would "knowingly" be taking the risk of having ADD children. This reinforced my need to say: "Enough!" We, who know firsthand how debilitating this disorder can be, cannot allow this pervasive mental condition to beat us or cheat us from continuing our lineage.

My newest goal involves demolishing this monster that compromises lives and destroys families. Anyone who has been touched personally by ADD will understand what fuels my passion for a cure. I hope I have inspired multitudes of concerned people to implore the mental health community to make this endeavor a reality. In the meantime, I am overwhelmingly thankful to have learned about the wondrous possibilities through dowsing.

As we end this remarkable year, one of unexpected discovery and change, Bob and I are healing our tattered past and look to new beginnings—without the struggles and stresses of ADD.

On the day we married, Bob said "grow old with me; the best is yet to be." I am not giving up on that ... ever.

EPILOGUE

It is now the winter of 2013, and I assume readers would appreciate a report on our progress. Terrific–thank you! Not perfect perhaps, but many light years away from our difficult past. It has been eighteen months since Bob's original healing, and we continue to experience opportunities to grow using our "miraculous discovery" in new and additional ways.

For example: although we already knew that proper blood flow and balancing the brain is crucial, we later realized that by including unawareness (one of Bob's worst ADD traits) to his daily therapeutic routine, the results were significantly more dramatic. Our "gift" seems to unfold in stages as we continue learning ... and loving our life together again.

This memoir was written to enlighten regarding ADD, its manifestations and repercussions.

For information on dowsing

The American Society of Dowsers
802-684-3417 - www.dowsers.org

Dowsing for ADD/ADHD
Basic Dowsing Technique
www.dowsers.org/add

BOOK CLUB QUESTIONS

1. Were you familiar with ADD but unaware of the devastation it can cause, especially to those who live with such a person?

2. What shocked you the most about what you read?

3. Did this change your overall perception of what it means to be afflicted with ADD?

4. What is your opinion on how Linda handled so many difficult circumstances over the decades?

5. Do you feel Linda could have or should have left Bob at any point?

6. Were you drawn in by Linda's confusion, pain, anger, and fear as she strived to do whatever she had to do to protect herself and her family?

7. Describe your feelings about Bob. Did you feel distain or sympathy for him—or both?

8. What was your take on the lack of help (and missed opportunities) from the mental health community to properly analyze Bob's issues, causing him a much delayed diagnosis?

9. How do you think Bob would have fared in life without Linda, his mentor/enabler?

10. Now that you have knowledge—and a list of symptoms—could you more readily recognize people close to you (or even acquaintances) as possibly having ADD?

11. If you were seriously involved in a relationship (but not married), then discovered that your partner had ADD—how would you react based on what you have read?

12. Were you stunned, amazed, spooked, or elated regarding the discovery that finally brought peace to this couple?

ACKNOWLEDGMENTS

In many situations, support from friends and family can make a significant difference. My supporters were indeed instrumental in keeping me tethered to the keyboard, often into the wee hours. They provided me reasons to keep writing ... even when I was sometimes unsure that it was the right thing to do.

In the beginning ... with just two (poorly drafted) chapters and tentative thoughts of continuing, it was Theodore R. DeRoche, Ph.D., LMHC who insisted I would be helping many thousands by writing this book. That appealed to my sense of sharing, and my journey began in earnest. Dr. DeRoche continued to cheer me on throughout this undertaking. Your support TR — priceless! Thank you.

I met Mary Lois Sanders, DMA, a well-respected editor, at a local writers group. She spurred me on—stating that my subject matter and writing style were indeed worthy of a book. Naturally, I hired her ... she believed in me, and my story! Her excellent ideas and concepts are incorporated into this final result. Thank you, Mary Lois.

Another local professional, Linda terBurg – author, publicist and advisor, overwhelmed me by describing the monumental tasks still ahead for marketing—then pitched right in to help! I appreciate you, Linda.

I am also appreciative of supportive friends and acquaintances. Many of you made excellent suggestions, especially when I read excerpts from the book. (You know who you are.) Cheerleaders all, I thrived on your enthusiasm.

I am especially grateful to Karen Durham and Tony and Mary Pedi, for leading me to "the discovery" that changed our life. If not for them connecting me to Raymon Grace, the ending of this book would have been quite different.

Bravo to Raymon Grace, the hero in my final chapter. He taught me that with an open mind ... anything is possible. I will never forget that lesson!

Finally ... big hugs to my devoted daughter, who held my hand through every step of this long process, and who, from the beginning, kept saying: "Keep writing, Mom—it's a riveting story that must be told."

Now to acknowledge the most important person of all: my husband Bob. In addition to endlessly performing as my in-house editor, he is the bravest man I know. Without his encouragement and sincere willingness to be exposed (as the villain), this important book would never have happened.

CPSIA information can be obtained at www.ICGtesting.com
Printed in the USA
LVOW061447050613

337131LV00016B/676/P